D1565115

*Practical Experience in
Building Expert Systems*

Practical Experience in Building Expert Systems

Edited by

Max Bramer
School of Information Science,
Portsmouth Polytechnic, UK

JOHN WILEY & SONS
Chichester · New York · Brisbane · Toronto · Singapore

Other Wiley Editorial Offices

John Wiley & Sons, Inc., 605 Third Avenue,
New York, NY 10158-0012, USA

Jacaranda Wiley Ltd, G.P.O. Box 859, Brisbane,
Queensland 4001, Australia

John Wiley & Sons (Canada) Ltd, 22 Worcester Road,
Rexdale, Ontario M9W 1L1, Canada

John Wiley & Sons (SEA) Pte Ltd, 37 Jalan Pemimpin # 05-04,
Block B, Union Industrial Building, Singapore 2057

Library of Congress Cataloging-in-Publication Data:

Practical experience in building expert systems / [edited by] Max
  Bramer.
    p.   cm.
  Includes bibliographical references.
  ISBN 0 471 92254 4
    1. Expert systems (Computer science)   I. Bramer, M. A. (Max A.)
  QA76.76.E95P73   1990
  006.3'3—dc20   89-27241
                                                            CIP

British Library Cataloguing in Publication Data:

Practical experience in building expert systems
  1. Expert systems
  I. Bramer, M. A.
  006.3'3

  ISBN 0 471 92254 4

Printed in Great Britain by Courier International, Tiptree, Essex

Contents

List of Contributors

JOHN ACKROFF   AT & T Bell Laboratories,
Warren,
New Jersey,
USA

PETER ALVEY   School of Medicine,
Royal Free Hospital,
London,
UK

MAX BRAMER   School of Information Science,
Portsmouth Polytechnic,
UK

IVAN BRATKO   Jožef Stefan Institute,
Ljubljana,
Yugoslavia

KEITH BRAUNWALDER   Hewlett-Packard,
Boise,
Idaho,
USA

GRAZIELLA BUTERA   Olivetti AI Center,
Ivrea,
Italy.

GARY CHAMBERLIN   City University,
London,
UK

CHAS CHURCH   Hitachi Europe Ltd,
London,
UK

MEL GREAVES   Leukaemia Research Fund Centre,
Institute of Cancer Research,
London,
UK

FEODORA HERRMANN   Hewlett-Packard,
Böblingen,
West Germany

MIKE KEEN   Expertech Ltd,
Slough,
Berkshire,
UK

NADA LAVRAČ   Jožef Stefan Institute,
Ljubljana,
Yugoslavia

RICHARD LELLIOTT   Sun Alliance,
Horsham,
Surrey,
UK

DIEGO LO GIUDICE   Olivetti AI Center,
Ivrea,
Italy.

ROB MILNE   Intelligent Applications Ltd,
Livingston,
West Lothian,
UK

IGOR MOZETIČ   Jožef Stefan Institute,
Ljubljana,
Yugoslavia

JESSICA RONCHI   Olivetti AI Center,
Ivrea,
Italy.

PAMELA SURKO   Science Applications International Corporation,
San Diego,
California,
USA

GREGG VESONDER   AT & T Bell Laboratories,
Warren,
New Jersey,
USA

JON WRIGHT   AT & T Bell Laboratories,
Warren,
New Jersey,
USA

STEFEK ZABA   Hewlett-Packard,
Bristol,
UK

1
Introduction

Max Bramer

The aim of this collection of case histories is to bring together the practical experience of a number of expert system developers from a variety of countries and working in a wide range of application areas.

Published descriptions of expert systems (ES) typically focus on either the technical details of the system itself or the financial benefits to its developer. Such accounts are of little value to the person who wishes to develop his or her own ES or who wishes to gain a general view of the state of the art of ES development at the practical level. This is the function that this volume seeks to fulfil; it attempts to answer questions such as:

— why were the key design decisions made?
— were they principled or *ad hoc*?
— which alternative approaches were considered and later abandoned?
— to what extent were decisions on software tools influenced by the availability of hardware?

and, more fundamentally,

— what are the lessons learnt that can be passed on to developers of future systems?

The ES field is currently characterized by a wide range of theoretical viewpoints, but an absence of generally accepted theory in many important areas. Opinions on the commercial value of ES vary from the extremely negative 'Expert Systems have failed' through to the dismissively positive 'Expert Systems are now routine in commercial applications'. There is a shortage of hard information, compounded by the widely varying definitions that seem to be applied.

In this book a broad interpretation of the term expert system is taken, extending beyond simple rule-based systems to those embodying more complex representations of human knowledge. With this interpretation there are undoubtedly many commercially successful applications (mainly rule-based) already in existence, but developing the more complex applications remains anything but routine.

Almost 25 years after the initial pioneering work (on Dendral) at Stanford University, building an ES remains a craft activity, performed by a still relatively small band of specialists, rather than an exact science, or an engineering discipline with a body of practice codified into a methodology.

In Britain, where rule-based shells running on PCs have gained a great deal of popularity, it has been claimed (notably by those who sell shells) that building an ES is a simple task which can easily be accomplished in a few days. A comparison of this with the development time of even quite routine Data Processing applications would seem to indicate that those making such claims view the range of possible ES applications as inherently narrow.

By contrast, those in the software engineering community have frequently regarded the development of ES as being just a minor extension of 'conventional' software engineering, with a slightly extended methodology.

The Artificial Intelligence (AI) research community from which ES technology was a spin-off in the early 1980s has frequently pointed to the inherent deficiencies of the rule-based programming paradigm (of which the AI community was originally the most fervent advocate) and has consequently adopted an ambivalent attitude to the commercial success of ES applications.

A further view is that a new discipline of Knowledge Engineering is emerging, which will need to be reconciled with techniques of software engineering but may be different in kind from them.

The practical evidence for these varying views is weak, often based more on prejudice or personal experience than on experimental evidence. With many of the most valuable commercial applications of ES technology likely to remain confidential and given the natural reluctance of system developers to talk about their failures and false starts as well as their successes this is hardly surprising.

It is hoped that this collection of case histories will contribute to the development of the now embryonic discipline of Knowledge Engineering by bringing together a collection of detailed descriptions of completed ES projects written from a critical viewpoint. Authors have been asked to describe their projects 'warts and all' and have responded well to this challenge.

The projects are completed in the sense of being finished, but not necessarily successfully so. Even those that appear technically successful may not be used in practice or be commercially worthwhile, so a number of partial or complete failures are described in this book, as well as several successes.

The focus is on identifying the underlying principles behind success or failure from the point of view of the potential developer asking the question: 'If I am starting or considering an ES project today, what should I know that will help me? What principles have emerged in the last five years that stop me from having to reinvent the wheel myself? What are the key factors that will determine whether or not I succeed?'.

No attempt has been made to select projects on the basis of either their size and complexity or their potential financial value. Of greater significance in soliciting contributions was the willingness of authors to discuss their experiences freely and candidly.

In the interests of facilitating comparison, both with each other and with other projects that may be known to the reader, authors were asked to write as far as possible to a standard format, which is reproduced as an appendix to this chapter. Most authors did not follow the format fully, but those items which were omitted may also be revealing.

It has been considered far more important to explain the reasons for decisions (which in some cases may be arbitrary), rather than to attempt to give a *post hoc* justification for each one. Projects have not been chosen to represent any particular technical or ideological viewpoint, although some bias of self-selection is no doubt inevitable. The most complex applications are no doubt under-represented, but those which are included represent a wide range of approaches, using a variety of hardware and software.

The applications described cover a wide range from medical diagnosis through process monitoring to interpretation of legislation and risk assessment for the insurance industry.

With one exception all the application areas described seem to have proved suitable for ES development. The exception is the strongly expressed view of Milne (Chapter 6) about process control: 'Although process control is widely considered an interesting area of activity for expert systems with a large number of projects in progress, our conclusions are that this is a very poor area for the application of expert systems, when the goal is a near-term success and a relatively easy development.'

The systems described vary from research vehicles to commercial systems in regular daily use. Development times varied from a few weeks for an early prototype to several years for the Leukaemia Diagnosis system described in Chapter 2.

Although the case histories should best speak for themselves, the following is a brief summary of some of the points that arise.

PERFORMANCE AIMS

An important distinction that emerges from these accounts is between those systems that are developed with the aim of performing correctly in all or nearly all possible cases (i.e. to be experts themselves) and those which are aimed at dealing with the relatively straightforward cases (say all but the hardest 10%), to free the human expert to concentrate personally on the most difficult ones.

It is obviously important for system developers to have a clear idea of their performance objectives. Keen (Chapter 5) states: 'the system would not act as a substitute for professional advice, which can take into account the peculiarities particularly of the more complex cases. To this end, it was intended that the system would concentrate on straightforward cases of employment law, recognizing the trickier areas of the law and advising the user to seek professional advice in such cases.'

By contrast Alvey and Greaves (Chapter 2) state: 'the difficult cases are crucial for any practical system in this field. Future users would not need assistance with the majority of simple cases—they would need help mainly on the very cases on which the pilot system [which correctly diagnosed about 70% of cases] was falling down ... high performance ... is the most important feature.'

The availability of human experts and the practicalities of the working environment in which the system will be used are obviously of great importance. Thus the availability of OCEX (Chapter 3) has freed order clearing experts to concentrate on the less than 1% of orders which the system cannot handle (because of the need for direct contact with the sales office or the customer) and this is regarded as a very acceptable outcome.

Developing a system which performs well on the relatively straightforward cases does not seem to have proved a problem in any of the projects described in this book, but to improve such a system to handle the most complex cases may involve a considerable increase in the effort required and may result in a much larger system, with a much more complex representation of knowledge.

The initial version of the Leukaemia Diagnosis system (Chapter 2) took only a short while to develop. Improving this system to achieve near-perfect performance took a further two and a half years.

The conclusion would seem to be that choosing to develop such high-performance systems may be essential in some fields and from an academic viewpoint may lead to greater insights into the problems of building ES, but can also lead to a considerable increase in the complexity of the task, with a much greater risk of failure and that companies entering the field might be better advised to look for applications where correctly handling say 80 to 90% of cases would be a valuable way of freeing human experts' time. It could also be argued that the human expert is likely to find this approach considerably less threatening and thus may be more likely to cooperate in system development.

KNOWLEDGE REPRESENTATION AND CHOICE OF DEVELOPMENT ENVIRONMENT

The systems described employ a number of representations, although most are predominantly rule-based.

KANT (Chapter 8) adopts a more complex representation in the form of a blackboard architecture supporting a collection of cooperating rule-based systems and Keen (Chapter 5) describes an approach to structuring a system by breaking it down into a number of separate knowledge bases.

KARDIO (Chapter 10) differs from the other systems in making use of a combination of deep and shallow knowledge, the former represented by means of a qualitative model.

The systems vary in size from a few hundred rules up to over 8000 Prolog clauses for KARDIO, the most complex of the systems described.

The choice of software for systems development varied from shells (some commercially available on PCs, others purely research vehicles), to versions of both Lisp and Prolog, to the AI development system KEE, running on a workstation.

The use of PC-based shells for ES development is a controversial area. Although several of the systems described in this volume were successfully implemented using shells, others seem to have found them too limited.

In some cases, such as KANT (Chapter 8) systems were developed in the same environment in which they were delivered to their users. In other cases, such as the Aries club project, different development and delivery environments were chosen.

Church (Chapter 4) comments: 'In the main, development within the intended delivery environment is still our general practice and avoids many of the complications (or impossibilities) of porting an application from development to delivery environment. Nevertheless, and for a widening range of applications, the promise of developing within a powerful workstation environment and then delivering on a cost-effective run-time environment is becoming a reality.'

He also points to the value of domain-specific rather than general shells to support particular classes of ES development.

KNOWLEDGE ACQUISITION

Knowledge Acquisition has often been described as the major bottleneck in ES development, but does not seem to have caused any serious difficulties in the case histories described in this book.

In most cases a single expert served as the knowledge source and Alvey and Greaves (Chapter 2) regard this as of crucial importance: 'The system has always been based on just one expert and this is the only practical basis for a system that must cover the whole of its field without any errors, omissions or duplications in the logic. Any occasional suggestions from other sources are always referred to the expert, who makes the final decision about what goes into the system. Trying to incorporate the views of a committee of experts in any other way would probably be disastrous: it would add little to the comprehensiveness and jeopardize the consistency of the system.'

Keen (Chapter 5) refers to the case where a second expert was introduced into a project, leading to fundamental disagreements with the original expert: 'these were resolved by the two experts talking the issues through with the knowledge engineer to reach a common agreed point of view. As part of this process of resolving differences, actually amending the existing system was found to be a useful way of showing one expert the ideas being put forward by the other.'

Relatively unsophisticated approaches to knowledge acquisition have generally been followed, largely based on unstructured interviewing techniques, with some mention of protocol analysis and of observation to augment interviewing.

However the interpretation placed on the knowledge acquisition process varied considerably. In the case of the second version of the Leukaemia Diagnosis project (Chapter 2), the knowledge acquisition is described as being 'done by apprenticeship', with the knowledge engineer almost becoming a domain expert in his own right after a lengthy series of discussions with the expert.

Keen (Chapter 5) paints the opposite picture, of the expert producing the first draft of the rules almost unaided and effectively learning to be his own knowledge engineer.

Milne (Chapter 6) describes the natural extension of these two approaches where the expert and the knowledge engineer are the same person, stai ng that: 'only the process engineer knew enough about the process to develop the knowledge base. Fortunately, this person was also trained in expert systems and as a result the knowledge base was developed from his own personal experience.'

Ackroff, Surko, Vesonder and Wright (Chapter 11) describe the process involved as more 'knowledge creation' than knowledge acquisition, since the knowledge engineer and domain expert needed to rework the expert's knowledge into a form that had never previously existed.

Although machine learning has been strongly advocated in some quarters as a means of circumventing problems of knowledge acquisition, the only system which made use of machine learning techniques was KARDIO (Chapter 10). This system used inductive learning to compress a large set of cases into rule form and, in this one case history at least, this technique would seem to have proved very successful.

USER INTERFACE

A great deal of effort has obviously been expended on developing good (generally graphically oriented) user interfaces. However, some caution may be necessary. Herrmann (Chapter 3) comments: 'When first designing the user interface for OCEX we planned to use a bit-mapped display to offer a graphically oriented user interface. We asked the users and they wanted a "very simple, form based user interface similar to those applications they have been using so far and which are available on a character terminal".'

Church (Chapter 4) remarks 'In the main I now assume that users are relatively unadventurous'.

Again it is necessary to consider in advance the user for whom the system is being developed. Although in most cases the user is likely to be at a level of skill well below that of the expert whose knowledge was built into the system, this is not always the case. For example, the Equity Selection System (Chapter 9) was constructed on the assumption that the user would be a well qualified expert in his own right. In recognition of the likelihood of different classes of user, the AutoTest-2 system (Chapter 11) incorporates separate interfaces for three classes of user 'basic users', 'advanced users' and 'administrators'.

The provision of good explanatory facilities for the user (generally based on tracing through rules) is normally considered to be an important part of ES design. In practice explanatory facilities are often also of great use to both the expert and the system builder during system development (Keen (Chapter 5) gives an illustration of this).

In the case of OCEX (Chapter 3) where the users did not require any explanation facility, additional facilities to support maintenance of the knowledge base by the end user were added to compensate.

Since one use of the explanation facilities is likely to be by the inexperienced user to gain basic familiarization with the system, Keen (Chapter 5) found it more convenient to incorporate a separate training package for inexperienced users.

The use of ES in a training role (as well as for their primary purpose of performing a given task) is also mentioned by some of the other authors. For example, KANT (Chapter 8) is now being used by the experts to train new staff, making use of the system's detailed explanation facilities.

Although not yet widely recognized as a valuable fringe benefit of building an ES, this use may be of increasing importance in the future.

REASONING WITH UNCERTAINTY

A particularly striking feature of the entire collection of case histories is the small part played by the 'traditional' techniques of reasoning with uncertainty (Bayesian reasoning, belief functions, possibility theory etc.) which not only are widely believed to be fundamental to ES development but which form one of the most hotly disputed areas of theoretical research.

It might have been predicted that such problems would loom large, but in practice they seem to have been of little importance, in some cases because there was no uncertainty in the domain, in others because uncertainty was dealt with by a variety of non-numerical approaches which seem to have proved adequate.

Alvey and Greaves (Chapter 2) have attempted to deal with

uncertainty in the same way as they believe experts do, by using qualifications such as 'definitely', 'possibly', 'compatible with' etc. They are disdainful of numerically based approaches to uncertainty, commenting: 'We have never been able to understand the fatal fascination of others for numerical toys. Their biggest effect—perhaps their only effect—is to cut you off from the most potent debugging aid of all— the expert.' Whatever the truth of this assertion, the collection of case histories as a whole casts considerable doubt on the practical value of research into numerical approaches to reasoning with uncertainty.

PROTOTYPING

There is widespread agreement on the value of prototyping and of producing the first prototype early.

For example, Ronchi, Butera and Lo Giudice (Chapter 8) state: 'In developing an expert system we believe that producing initially a huge pile of specifications is meaningless. The specifications come out during the prototype development, and only when the prototype is complete are the specifications outlined and almost clear.'

Braunwalder and Zaba (Chapter 7) illustrate the further benefit of iterated prototyping in gaining and retaining acceptance from both subject experts and management: '... each stage of prototyping had visible deliverables and resolved a particular area of uncertainty identified in the feasibility investigation. These frequent checkpoints also provided demonstrable progress, important both to sustain the interest of the experts providing the critical knowledge, and to reassure management that some return was likely on the investment of effort.'

Herrmann (Chapter 3) also reports that an early prototype supports the involvement and cooperation of end users, quoting the remark: 'You wrote a prototype within only three weeks. When we saw what is possible with that new expert system technology we were convinced that this approach will solve our problems!'.

Alvey and Greaves (Chapter 2) make the point that design decisions made in a prototype should not necessarily be retained unaltered in later versions: 'the factor that has probably contributed most to the success of the project is the willingness to dig up the foundations at frequent intervals.'

The experience of Alvey and Greaves also indicates that a straightforward progression cannot necessarily be assumed between a reasonably successful prototype and a fully correct system. The latter may take considerably more effort than the former and involve a major change of representation.

Ackroff, Surko, Vesonder and Wright (Chapter 11) warn that the path from prototype to finished product may be far from simple: 'In our view, expert system projects fail too frequently because they cannot escape the prototype stage. The most frequent reason is a failure on the part of the developers to provide a viable migration path to product. The time between the completion of the prototype and the availability of the product version is the key variable.'

FACTORS AFFECTING ACCEPTABILITY

Not all the systems described in this volume were developed with routine use as a major aim. For example, the Aries Club project (Chapter 9) was principally concerned with promoting awareness of ES technology within the UK insurance industry and thus sought to develop two systems as prototypes, rather than for immediate operational use. In the case of the one system developed by a software house purchase by customers was taken as the indicator of success, rather than everyday use.

The systems which did find immediate acceptance in practical use were those developed in companies to fulfil a specific aim. In these cases acceptability was assured assuming the systems performed the intended task to an appropriate standard.

Such systems also automatically fitted into the existing hardware and software environments of the company as they were developed internally.

Church (Chapter 4) describes the transition of ES from being isolated advisors to systems fully integrated with an organization's existing software as being one of the key factors in their growing commercial acceptance. For this reason he regards it as important for the system to fit into the user's existing hardware environment. When a system is originally developed on different hardware 'the integration work has often overshadowed the expert systems implementation in terms of both difficulty and time'.

Alvey and Greaves (Chapter 2) stress the importance of an enthusiastic expert and the experience of Ronchi, Butera and Lo Giudice with KANT (Chapter 8) illustrates the perils of working with an expert who is not committed to the project. Their experts 'were not very convinced about our AI approach. Their fear was of losing their job. Our impression is that they did not themselves perceive the need for a knowledge-based approach but they were forced by their manager. ... They were ... often not available. Often they gave us books and technical documents to read instead of explaining and helping us in understanding and modelling the knowledge.'

Several other contributors point to the importance of involving the user at an early stage and Braunwalder and Zaba (Chapter 7) suggest that this should be as early as possible 'since the early "technology proving" phases would be determined more by the feasibility of the desirable rather than trying to make the feasible useful'. Milne (Chapter 6) deliberately took another approach for his rotating machinery system: 'In order to ensure that the end users did not become disenchanted with the system, they were not exposed to it until we were happy that the systems test and final test efforts had been completed.'

Braunwalder and Zaba (Chapter 7) point out that even implementing a successful prototype does not guarantee acceptance: 'one of the dangers of demonstrating good performance on the low-volume product proved to be fears from some people responsible for ... the higher-volume product that differences between the two products meant it would not be possible to use the same approach.'

Expert systems projects can fail for a variety of organizational reasons. Milne (Chapter 6) states: 'The organizational issues were the dominating factors on the success and failures of all the projects we have been involved with .... In the first [unsuccessful] project, the expectation of the management was not consistent with the understanding of the problem by the technical team .... Another major organizational problem is the lack of ability of those companies to calculate the exact return on investment. ... Essentially the organization did not understand in quantitative terms what its problem was.'

In Milne's machinery monitoring example it was necessary to take into account the expectations of several very diverse groups of users. He comments 'It was not possible to judge ahead of time what a machinery diagnostic system meant to many of the potential users .... It is important to realize that the potential end users never look at the specification or the agreed limitations of the system. They had a pre-conceived notion of what it should do, and that was exactly what it must do.'

One of the paradoxes of expert system development is that although making an expert's knowledge explicit is one of the principal benefits of using ES technology for many applications, for others it may be most unwelcome for reasons of confidentiality. This was one of the problems in the case of the Equity Selection System developed for the Aries Club project (Chapter 9): 'As work progressed, it proved necessary to limit the depth [of the system], in order to preserve confidentiality of the most detailed expertise .... The lead expert's nervousness over releasing confidential knowledge increased during the course of the project.'

Psychological factors can also play an important part. Bratko, Lavrač and Mozetič (Chapter 10) report that the principal lesson learned from their work was how difficult it is to actually introduce a medical expert system into routine clinical use: '... in addition to the technical merit, the psychological factor is decisive for accepting such a medical expert system into routine practice. The potential manufacturer, also worried about the legal liability, normally consults domain specialists ... for opinion. The opinion of the specialists is typically reserved. The reasons ... are in our experience largely irrational and stem from viewing an expert system as a competitor. ... In the task of diagnosis which is ... believed to be really their exclusive domain. The task of diagnosis is perceived as one requiring highest intellectual skill, experience and intuition, and is impossible to explain and therefore impossible to mechanize. Objective, measurable technical criteria, such as diagnostic accuracy, are of minor importance in this argument.'

APPENDIX—OUTLINE STRUCTURE FOR EACH CASE HISTORY

Abstract
A brief summary of what the system does, how it was built and what was achieved.

(1) *Introduction*
Brief details of who you are, where and when the project was done etc.

(2) *Objectives*
What were you trying to do? The nature of the problem to be solved. How would success be measured (e.g. financial benefit)?

(3) *Systems Specification*
Scope of the problem and context within the organization. Who produced the specification? How did it alter as the project progressed? What were the evaluation criteria at the start of the project?

(4) *Use of Resources*
What is the hardware and software environment for the system? How were the hardware and software selected? Integration with

other software (e.g. databases, spreadsheets, mathematical models). How were staff recruited and trained? What design method was used (e.g. prototyping, formal specification)? How were staff organized (e.g. into project teams)? Development v delivery environments.

(5) *Involvement of Users*
At what stages? What was their role?

(6) *Knowledge Acquisition*
How did you acquire the knowledge (e.g. interviewing, protocol analysis, induction)? How did you deal with conflicts between multiple experts? How readily available was the expert knowledge? What was the experts' reaction to the knowledge elicitation process?

(7) *Representation and Reasoning*
What 'high-level' model of the problem did you construct? What representation did you choose and why? How did you deal with uncertainty in representation and reasoning and why? Quantitative summary (e.g. number of facts, rules, metarules).

(8) *User Interface*
What sort of user model was implemented, if any? What explanation facilities were provided? What use was made of natural language, graphics, mice, interactive video etc?

(9) *Evaluation*
Performance versus objectives? Evaluation of value to the organization? At what stage was evaluation carried out? As a result of this evaluation, what would you do differently/the same in future? Has the system been used in practice? Current state? What future developments are planned?

(10) *Organizational Issues*
The politics of introducing innovation? How did the project originate? Motivation and background? How were funding and approval obtained? How was the project managed? Was there support from top management throughout? Timescales? How important is the application to the organization (fairly helpful, helpful, ... , essential)—tactical versus strategic. Why was the AI approach used? How influenced was the decision to adopt an AI approach by peer group pressure? How did the organization gain its AI knowledge initially? How is the maintenance of the knowledge base envisaged?

(11) *Lessons Learnt*
Reasons for success/failure. What were the major bottlenecks (technical and/or organizational)? How 'principled' were the decisions described in Sections (2)–(9)? What would you change if you were doing this project again?

(12) *Personal Comments*
Any other points you wish to make.

(13) *Conclusions*

(14) *References*

2

The Leukaemia
Diagnosis Project

Peter Alvey and Mel Greaves

ABSTRACT

The Leukaemia Diagnosis System was designed to assist with the precise
diagnosis of leukaemia cases by interpreting the results from the latest
laboratory tests. Only a limited number of immunologists have the
experience required to give a comprehensive interpretation of these
specialized tests and the system has been based on the expertise of one
of them.

Knowledge elicitation was by unstructured interviews and the system
was built as a logic program—with knowledge represented in ordinary
Prolog structures and managed by highly specialized tools designed
specifically for their tasks.

The system is currently at the stage of an 'in house' working prototype.
It gives conclusions, reasons and suggestions for extra tests that may
improve the conclusions, and it performs satisfactorily on 400 past
cases—including many difficult or rare cases. Further development and

objective evaluation are in progress, in preparation for a version to be used in other centres.

INTRODUCTION

The Leukaemia Diagnosis Project started as a small study into the problems and feasibility of using knowledge-based methods in a specialized area of medical diagnosis. As the work progressed, it became increasingly clear that it had considerable potential value beyond its theoretical origins, and it has been progressively expanded into a practical system.

The project was initiated in late 1982–early 1983, at the Imperial Cancer Research Fund, London WC2, where all the participants were working at the time. It is based on the expertise of immunologist Mel Greaves, who is now the Director of the Leukaemia Research Fund Centre, at The Institute of Cancer Research, London SW3. The early work was done by Chris Myers, a graduate student in his laboratory, and he built a pilot system using EMYCIN, under the supervision of John Fox (Fox *et al* 1985).

When Chris Myers moved to the USA in early 1984, the subsequent development of the system was taken over by Peter Alvey, a former surgeon with previous experience of medical expert systems and logic programming. This second phase resulted in a substantial high performance prototype system, running on the ICRF DEC-20 mainframe computer, and the major problems of the project were overcome during this period.

The third phase is the development of a microcomputer version, which has been undertaken at the Royal Free Hospital School of Medicine since January 1987, supported by Grant No. 87/12 from the Leukaemia Research Fund. The micro-based system is currently being extended with the latest domain knowledge and after further evaluation it should be suitable for general use.

OBJECTIVES

The aim of the program is to interpret the latest laboratory tests used in the diagnosis of leukaemia. These are based mainly on monoclonal antibodies, which are extremely specific chemicals that can recognize and stain particular types of cell. A sample of the patient's blood or bone marrow is tested with a range of monoclonal antibodies and this results in a table of the percentage of cells in the sample recognized by each individual antibody (or with difficult cases the antibodies are sometimes used in pairs). An experienced immunologist can deduce from this information which type of blood cell is forming the basis of the leukaemia and this may be very important in selecting the best treatment for the patient. There are many different types of leukaemia and the results of treatment have improved dramatically over the last 10 to 15 years. This is due in some part to the selection of the most appropriate treatment for each particular type of the disease.

However, the interpretation of the monoclonal marker results is not simple. It would be nice if there were 'magic' markers that individually signified each type of leukaemia, but unfortunately this is rarely the case; it is only combinations of positive results that achieve significance. Furthermore, most of the markers are found on normal blood cells of the various types, as well as their leukaemic counterparts, and samples from healthy individuals would yield positive results for many of the tests. Thus the interpretation of the results has two components: deducing which types of cell are predominant in the sample, and deciding whether those cells are normal or leukaemic. It is even possible for mixtures of different cell types to be present and any or all of them may be involved with the leukaemia.

In some cases it cannot be decided from the test results whether the patient has leukaemia or not and the report sent to the clinicians might then be something like: 'Immature B cells are present in the sample, and if you have other information to indicate that the patient has leukaemia, then the sub-type of the leukaemia would be Common Acute Lymphoblastic Leukaemia'. (In the early system this would be abbreviated to 'compatible with Common ALL', but too concise a knowledge representation has subsequently caused serious problems.) The objective is not only to distinguish leukaemia from normality, but also from a wide range of simple illnesses. Infections like influenza can cause a considerable increase in the number of B cells in the blood (these make antibodies to fight the infection) but it would be disastrous if they were mistaken for the components of a B cell leukaemia. In both conditions there would be abnormal results for the relevant marker tests but it is important to recognize which is which.

In many cases the significance of the monoclonal marker results is clear-cut, even to the novice in the field, but in other cases the opposite is true, and considerable knowledge of the underlying biology may be required for an appropriate interpretation. As leukaemia is not a common disease there are few people in the world who have had the experience necessary to give the best interpretation on every case that comes along. This situation is unlikely to change because this branch of science is proceeding at a rapid rate and relevant discoveries are being made week by week. Only those experts at the heart of the research can keep pace with the rapidly changing state of knowledge.

Most cases of leukaemia are presented to hospitals remote from research centres. The antibodies required for immunodiagnostic screening are commercially available and it is quite feasible for the local hospitals to perform most of the diagnostic marker tests—but interpretation of the results is another matter. The objective of the project is clearly to provide assistance for the diagnosis of leukaemia in such hospitals and to make the skill of one experienced immunologist available for the benefit of the greatest number of patients. As a secondary benefit the system may also provide a useful research tool through the consistency of its conclusions, which could be an important factor in the trials required to find better treatments for this disease.

The success of the final system would not easily be measured, partly because the results of monoclonal antibody tests are only one component of the decision making process. In many cases the system may only confirm the diagnosis that would have been reached without it, but occasionally it may indicate a situation that could not otherwise have been detected. However, it would not need to save many patients from receiving a sub-optimal treatment before its benefits would be regarded as substantial.

SYSTEM SPECIFICATION

The project started as a humble exercise in knowledge acquisition and only when the pilot system showed useful potential was a more substantial system planned. There was no formal specification for the system but the straightforward nature of its task did not really require one. The input data consist of a set of clinical and laboratory data that is known when the program is run and the output is a fairly simple conclusion for the case. Little else is relevant. Users will not want to start a dialogue with the system and we soon adopted the practice of always giving a concise explanation or justification of the conclusion, regardless of whether the user wants it.

When the main prototype system was being developed the principal concern was the achievement of high performance. Without this the whole project would have failed—because of the nature of the overall task—so little thought was given to features other than the acquisition and representation of the domain. When this was well under way, convenient ways of adding explanations and further test recommendations virtually suggested themselves and were easily added to the system.

The evaluation criteria are also quite simple: the degree with which the conclusions of the system agree with those of the expert on whom it is based. These are necessarily somewhat subjective, and they also evolve a little as the expert's knowledge increases, but measurement is not a problem at any particular time. There is no objective way to know if the answers are correct in any absolute sense, because the subject is so close to the frontiers of science. Only time will tell whether today's theories continue to hold their value; but by that time the system will have been modified in the light of newer ones.

WHAT WAS DONE

The pilot system

The pilot system was based upon knowledge gained from protocol analysis and from the system builder's personal knowledge of the field. The expert gave a running commentary as he formed opinions on a training set of 67 cases. This was recorded on tape and the 'nuggets' of knowledge were highlighted from the resulting transcripts and extracted. They were incorporated into EMYCIN rules and a substantial amount of refinement was required to produce a plausible system. Its conclusions were simply the diagnostic category into which the case was assigned, and the only qualification for the conclusions was the final EMYCIN certainty factor. This did not correspond to any of the terms used by the expert ('probably', 'possibly', 'compatible with', etc) but attempting to match these would have been unreasonable for a demonstrator system. Numerical certainty factors other than 1 (or −1) were used in the EMYCIN rules but both the system builder and the expert would probably agree that there was little rational basis for the values selected.

The pilot system achieved its objective of demonstrating the feasibility of the project. On a separate test set, 70% of its crude conclusions agreed with the corresponding component of the expert's opinions and it was clearly impressive that it should get so many cases right. However, the burning question remained: what must be done to convert it into a practical system that would get the other 30% right as well? Did it need more rules of the same type, or was a radical new approach required?

Analysis of the pilot system

To determine the best way to proceed, a thorough analysis of the pilot system was undertaken. Its completeness and consistency was examined rule by rule and questions were asked about what went wrong when it gave a poo. conclusion. The results were very illuminating and have been reported in detail elsewhere (Alvey, Myers and Greaves 1987). Basically, the stumbling block was the existence in the test set of a hard core of difficult cases. They numbered only 5% of the sample and were either examples of rare conditions or cases with atypical features, eg false negative or false positive test results. Such cases do, however, occur in real life and any set of leukaemia cases could be expected to have a small but distinct proportion of difficult cases. The pilot system failed to handle these cases because of their complexity. It only had a superficial view of the domain and had no notion of false positive or false negative test results or of exceptions to general rules. Nor did it need to know of such things to diagnose the great majority of simple cases correctly.

However, the difficult cases are crucial for any practical system in this field. Future users would not need assistance with the majority of simple cases—they would need help mainly on the very cases on which the pilot system was falling down. In other applications high performance may not be quite so important but in this, and probably other medical applications, it is the most important feature.

Building the practical system

The clear message from the analysis was that a large system could not be grafted onto the old pilot system—a completely new start was required. On the second time round, however, the objectives and, more importantly, the motivation were different. We had to get the difficult cases right at all costs. Getting a few correct answers was not enough and the early rules had to form a sound foundation on which more complex rules could subsequently be based. Whenever the later rules would not fit in easily, the earlier rules were changed and the factor that has probably contributed most to the success of the project is the willingness to dig up the foundations at frequent intervals.

The new system was written as a tree structured logic program in Prolog and domain specific tools were written to manage the patient data and perform the rather specialized logical operations on it. New knowledge was acquired from the expert by unstructured interviews but, more importantly, an understanding of the domain was sought—not just titbits of knowledge to be handled at arm's length. It was quite clear that the project would not succeed unless the system builder himself could understand why a difficult case was difficult, in the terms of the domain.

The new knowledge and understanding was obtained at 2 to 3 hour sessions every 4 to 6 weeks and the system was progressively rebuilt. It was tested on the same 100 case test set used for the pilot system but an exact correspondence with the expert's qualified conclusions was sought. The new system could get up to 83% of the cases right quite rapidly but going beyond that level proved very difficult. Time after time changes to the rules would correct the problem in hand but cause other cases to be diagnosed incorrectly, when previously they had been correct. All the time, however, the representation of the domain was getting more detailed, and eventually the system was able to give a satisfactory conclusion for all 100 cases.

The process was repeated with three more sets of 100 cases each, but the third and fourth test sets did not require any significant changes to the rules. After two and a half years work we had a system that would handle almost any case—difficult ones as well as easy ones (Alvey, Preston and Greaves 1987).

USE OF RESOURCES

The pilot system was built in EMYCIN on a DEC-20, for the simple reason that both were available and already in use at the time. EMYCIN proved adequate for this small part of the task but previous experience had shown it to be too restrictive a format for large systems (Alvey 1983). The second phase of the system was written in Edinburgh University DEC-10 Prolog because that too was already available.

The third phase of the project—still in progress—is the transfer to microcomputers (with further developments). This was inevitable once it became clear that the program would have a useful practical value. LPA Prolog Professional was selected for the micro-system because it is a powerful Prolog from a firm with considerable experience of logic programming. The development work is done on IBM-compatible microcomputers but in principle it should be transferable to any other computer that will run LPA Prolog, with sufficient memory.

For most of the project the staffing has consisted of one system builder, having consultations with the expert and occasional advice from colleagues. For one year (1985) we had the services of a support programmer, Nicola Preston, who contributed a user-friendly interface for the DEC-20 system.

INVOLVEMENT OF USERS

Now that the performance problems have been resolved and a preliminary microcomputer version is running, we are starting to test the system in the immunology laboratories of close collaborators. In due course the circle of collaborators will be extended and eventually we hope the system can be used in a large number of hospitals.

The program is not yet complete—some major revisions are still being made to the domain rules—but its current state is suitable for obtaining useful feedback from close collaborators. Already some differences in laboratory practices have been identified and the interaction may indicate the need for additional facilities such as a 'what if' mechanism or an elaborate management system for database files.

KNOWLEDGE ACQUISITION

For the pilot system the knowledge elicitation was by protocol analysis with some further clarifications from the expert—and the system builder's own knowledge of the domain undoubtedly contributed to the process. However, it is interesting to look back at the rules of the pilot system with the understanding gained from making the subsequent system.

Two things stand out. Firstly, there was a lack of structure in the elicited knowledge. The rules were each satisfactory in their own right but they tended to go straight from raw data to conclusion in very few steps and various important intermediate concepts or subgroupings were missed. It was a question of not seeing the wood for the trees: the methods used had elicited the trees but not the wood.

Secondly there were one or two flaws in the elicited knowledge that caused performance problems. In retrospect it is easy to see how they arose—they were in fact unkind traps for the unwary, and they must be regarded as a normal hazard of knowledge elicitation. The practical observation is that they could so easily have been avoided—simply by asking the expert!

For the large scale system the knowledge acquisition was done by apprenticeship. The early discussions concentrated on the underlying biology of leukaemia and an understanding was sought of the important factors on which the diagnostic process is based. Inevitably this could not all be taken in at once and was built up over many months, even years. Probably the most important factor was the willingness of the expert and the knowledge engineer to go over the same ground time and time again, often from different viewpoints. For those who insist on relating everything to pre-existing categories, it would be closest to say that knowledge acquisition was by unstructured interviews—but that misses the point.

The system has always been based on just one expert and this is the only practical basis for a system that must cover the whole of its field without any errors, omissions or duplications in the logic. Any occasional suggestions from other sources are always referred to the expert, who makes the final decision about what goes into the system. Trying to incorporate the views of a committee of experts in any other way would probably be disastrous: it would add little to the comprehensiveness and jeopardize the consistency of the system. More importantly, it would destroy its identity. The expert is a very enthusiastic supporter of the project and reacts very favourably to having his logic encoded in this way—as most other experts do. This degree of motivation could only diminish in a hybrid system. We shall be studying the range of views of other experts as a separate investigation and, of course, we can modify the system in the light of any interesting findings, but the program will remain a single expert system.

REPRESENTATION AND REASONING

The system is written as a decision tree using the built-in Horn clause logic of Prolog. The microcomputer version has 1807 clauses, roughly half of which are domain rules and the remainder are tools for handling the patient data and all the procedural aspects of running a consultation.

A decision tree structure was used because this was the way that the expert used to explain how he analyses a case. It was simple and natural to link all the little decision trees into one large tree to represent the whole system. As time went by, this structure became more and more important as major sections of the program needed to be rewritten to reflect the better understanding of the domain. The structure enabled the relevant rules to be found easily and their interrelationships—with themselves and with other groups of rules—to be seen. Controlling these interactions is the vital factor for ensuring the completeness and consistency of the overall system.

Explanations are built into the individual rules and so too is the mechanism for making the suggestions for extra tests that may be of benefit. There would be no general way of making explanations to suit the intelligence and tolerance of the eventual users. Many results have to be screened during the logic, and explanations including all the items that were examined but proved to be non-contributory would defeat their purpose. Very many details are omitted from the explanations; sometimes it is the positive results that are left out, sometimes the negative or unknown values. There is no consistent pattern and, in this domain, the explanations have to be hand crafted within the individual rules, which are thus IF–THEN–BECAUSE rules or IF–THEN–BECAUSE–SUGGEST rules.

Uncertainty is handled in the same way that the expert handles it— by using qualifications such as: 'definitely', 'possibly', 'compatible with', applied to the categories that are concluded. This is all that is required and it enables the expert to help track down the problems when the system goes wrong. We have never been able to understand the fatal fascination of others for numerical toys. Their biggest effect—perhaps their only effect—is to cut you off from the most potent debugging aid of all—the expert. He can usually spot the cause of a particular problem—but not if the system uses an alien and arcane method of computation.

USER INTERFACE

Only a simple user interface is needed in this application. The table of clinical details and laboratory test results is entered at the start of the consultation and the system displays the conclusion for the case on the screen and puts it into a file for subsequent printout. A concise explanation of the conclusion is always given next, with progressive indentation of the nested sub-reasons, which are written in the jargon of the haematologist/immunologist (see Figure 2.1).

The explanation is followed by the suggestions for any extra tests that might improve the certainty of the conclusion, and these are restricted to those that are immediately relevant. This is probably the most useful feature of the system since it is rarely possible to do all of the potentially useful tests on the first round: in some cases there may only be a small quantity of the blood or bone marrow sample. The system always gives a conclusion, however many tests have been performed, and analysis of small samples can be done in several stages with the system's test suggestions guiding the choice of tests for each subsequent round.

Computer Diagnosis for pt-5124 test-1 :-

UNCLASSIFIABLE
   because TDT MARKERS are negative
         because TDT =< 5
   and MYELOID markers are unclassifiable
         because MYELOID and PRE-T markers occur on the same cells
               because CD33 + CD7 > 120%
               and MYELOID positivity might only be on Pre-T cells
                   because CD5 > 20
                   and MYELOID & T lineage markers
                               could be on the same cells
                       because CD33//CD5 is unknown
   and early lymphoid cell type is: unknown
         because Pre-T markers are unclassifiable
               because CD7 +ve cells may be myeloid
               because 1 MYELOID marker
                         occurs on the CD7 +ve cells
                       because CD33 + CD7 > 120%
               and there are fewer than 2
                            corroborative T markers
                 because CD5 + CD7 > 120%
                   and CD1 & CD2 & CD3 & CD4 &
                             CD8 + CD7 =< 120%
                   and CD3cyt is unknown
   and early myeloid cell type is: unclassifiable
         because non-specific myeloid cells are not assessable
         because MYELOID markers are unclassifiable
   and monocytes are not present
         because SMIG =< 20

Further test suggestions for pt-5124 test-1 :-
   CD33//CD5 . . to detect T lineage & MYELOID markers on the
          same cells

   WT1//CD3cyt . to corroborate the PRE-T marker

                Clinical Data for pt-5124 Sample: test-1

AGE 68   BLAST.COUNT . . . 85
SEX . . . . FEMALE   WBC 3.3
CLINICAL DIAGNOSIS . ALL   MEDIASTINAL MASS . ABSENT
SAMPLE TYPE . . . . MARROW

Figure 2.1 (for caption, see p. 26)

```
                    Marker Test Results (%)

CD1 (NA134)  . 0    CD7  (WT1)   . . 91   DA2 . . . . . . 18
CD2 (OKT11A) . 0    CD8  (C3)  . . . 4    JO . . . . . . . 0
CD3 (T28)  . . 2    CD10 (AL2) . . 0      SHEEP-ROSETTES . 0
CD4 (OKT4) . . 10   CD13 (MY7) . . 3      SMIG . . . . . . 5
CD5 (S33)  . . 45   CD33 (MY906) . 57     TDT . . . . . . 5
```

Figure 2.1   Example of the system's output for a difficult case

In this case there is evidence of leukaemia (BLAST COUNT 85%) but there are at least some cells that have markers for two different types of leukaemia. There is insufficient evidence to decide whether it is a case of pre-T cell acute lymphoblastic leukaemia (T-ALL) with a false negative TDT and a false positive CD33 or whether it is an acute myeloid leukaemia with false positive CD7 and CD5 markers. The tests suggested by the system are double marker tests that measure the proportion of cells with both markers present. With favourable results for these tests it might be possible to reach a firm conclusion, alternatively the case would be quite unclassifiable with the state of current scientific knowledge.

Note that a conclusion of 'UNCLASSIFIABLE because all my rules have failed' would be singularly unconvincing for professional users.

EVALUATION

Informal evaluation has been conducted throughout the development of the full system. As each new set of 100 cases was taken from store the current system's conclusions were compared with those of the expert. Once the system had been modified to give 'correct' answers for every one, it was retested on all previous test sets to check that its answers for them were still correct. With only a few trivial exceptions the performance on previous cases remained satisfactory so that the major fear of over-fitting the rules to any set of cases did not materialize. Currently a single version of the system will give a satisfactory conclusion for every case that has been used in the development, including the 400 test cases and several other difficult cases that have come into our laboratory during that period.

The assessment is done by the expert who has little difficulty in deciding whether he would be prepared to sign a report bearing the conclusion in question. This measure of performance is obviously the most relevant but, in addition, we are planning a blind trial to compare the system's conclusions with those of a panel of other experts in the field. The objective will be to compare the agreement of the system with the experts against the degree to which the experts agree amongst themselves.

LESSONS LEARNT

Two major lessons were learned from the project. The first is that high performance expert systems can only be based on a good understanding of the domain. Secondly, the implementation must allow for thorough debugging and frequent revisions of the whole system. The knowledge engineer cannot possibly obtain a good understanding of the domain at the outset and major changes to the overall plan of the system are inevitable, as his understanding evolves. Maintenance is the most critical requirement, and when we have a choice between different methods of knowledge representation, we always choose the one that is easiest to maintain.

The exact methods used for knowledge acquisition and implementation of the system probably do not matter; provided that the key requirements are met. There is a large element of personal variation in the learning process and in building maintainable systems, and it is probably best for the individuals concerned to use the methods that they are happiest with. Our methods worked well for us but they may not be the best for others.

PERSONAL COMMENTS

Although the project has broken substantial new ground, we are left with a curious feeling that the wheel has come full circle. In a way our work has re-invented the wheel of systems analysis, and also the wheel of software maintenance. We started with a knowledge-based approach but found that this does not provide any short cuts around the practicalities of programming real world applications.

The major problem with other expert systems is their propensity to give occasional stupid answers (Miller 1984). If you were to ask an experienced software engineer to design any type of system that avoided such blunders as its highest priority, then the last thing he would suggest would be to throw a few rules into an unstructured shell without any debugging aids. Yet that is what the early expert systems gurus have been urging others to do.

CONCLUSIONS

A substantial diagnostic system for assisting with leukaemia diagnosis has been programmed directly from human expertise. The application is small but very complex and a useful high performance system has been produced. After 5 person years of work it will soon be ready for field testing and we are optimistic that it will be of considerable practical use.

The major problem in its development was ensuring accuracy of all of its conclusions, for difficult cases as well as simple ones. This was eventually achieved by a methodical approach with painstaking attention to detail in two main areas: obtaining a good understanding of the domain, and a precise representation of this understanding in a form that can be maintained. Complex artificial intelligence techniques were not required because simple (but detailed) logic programming was tried first and proved to be adequate. Programming was not the limiting factor and the format of the system has been adapted to follow the changing specification of the task in a flexible way.

Despite the unsophisticated implementation, the program can fairly be described as an expert system, because the driving force behind all of its conclusions is the logic of the expert. There is nothing else inside it and, for maintainable high performance, that is what really counts.

REFERENCES

Alvey, P.L. (1983). The Problems of Designing a Medical Expert System. Proceedings of the Third Annual Conference of the British Computer Society Specialist Group on Expert Systems, pp. 30–42.

Alvey, P.L., Myers, C.D. and Greaves, M.F. (1987). High Performance for Expert Systems: I. Escaping from the Demonstrator Class. *Medical Informatics*, 12, 85–95.

Alvey, P.L., Preston, N.J. and Greaves, M.F. (1987). High Performance for Expert Systems: II. A System for Leukaemia Diagnosis. *Medical Informatics*, 12, 97–114.

Fox, J., Myers, C.D., Greaves, M.F. and Pegram, S. (1985). Knowledge Acquisition for Expert Systems: Experience in Leukaemia Diagnosis. *Methods of Information in Medicine*, 24, 65–72.

Miller, R.A. (1984). INTERNIST/CADUCEUS: Problems Facing Expert Consultant Programs. *Methods of Information in Medicine*, 23, 9–14.

3

OCEX—Order Clearing Expert System

Feodora Herrmann

ABSTRACT

OCEX (Order Clearing Expert System) checks orders for medical products by producing instructions on how to proceed with each order, e.g. corrective instructions for incorrect orders. The introduction of the expert system has led to dramatic quality improvements and considerable savings in order processing. Our experience has shown that the order clearing problem cannot be solved using 'conventional' software technologies.

INTRODUCTION

During recent years a considerable number of expert systems has been built, most of them by research institutes or major companies. The main goal was to learn and prove, with prototype applications, the usefulness, feasibility, and advantages of expert system technologies.

Even today, only a few expert systems have proven to be profitable in daily routine use. This means there is still little experience in objectives and requirements for commercial expert systems and how they can be built in a traditionally oriented information systems environment (Holsapple *et al* 1987, Mertens 1987).

Since April 1988, the expert system OCEX has been in daily use at Böblingen Medical Division, one of the Hewlett-Packard factories in Germany. OCEX is designed to check all orders arriving at the factory for correctness and completeness in configuration, and to guide the end user in the Order Processing Department with corrective actions. Design and successful implementation have been possible through the cooperation of two HP entities: first, implementation by the Information Systems Department; second, consultancy by a department whose focus is technology transfer for new software technologies as knowledge-based programming technologies.

Figure 3.1 summarizes the achievements accomplished by having implemented and introduced OCEX. They are described in more detail in this paper.

* saves money (ROI)

* in daily operational use

* underlying problem could not be solved using 'conventional' software technologies

* integrated in a commercial EDP environment

* knowledge base maintenance by the end users themselves

Figure 3.1   OCEX highlights

THE ORDER CLEARING PROBLEM

There is a trend in the manufacturing industry (mechanical engineering and electrical engineering) towards an increasing complexity of products. A basic product is generally offered, but the final product shipped to the customer is influenced by many factors: first, customer needs and wishes must be considered; second, market specific requirements characterize the product; and finally, factory internal procedures such

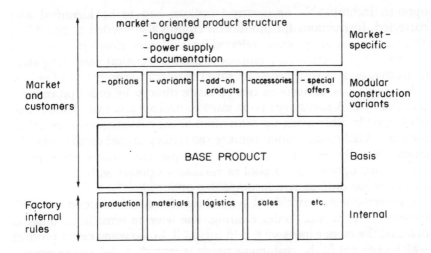

Figure 3.2   Factors influencing a product configuration

as production control or flow of materials and logistics affect a correct product configuration.

Examples of such complex products are the medical instruments manufactured and distributed by the Hewlett-Packard Böblingen Medical Division (BMD). When such an instrument is ordered, order options specify the exact configuration. These are:

— country specific options (e.g. power cable, language of documentation)

— product specific options (e.g. for special sensors; or cuff options; or arrhythmia options)

— sales options, which may be valid only for a certain period

— internal options, which must be added for production control purposes.

Some options are mutually exclusive or dependent on each other.

This complex system of options for medical instruments was the main reason for a high rate of order changes for these products. Also, knowledge changes frequently due to introduction of new products and marketing programs, therefore it is difficult for sales staff to keep their knowledge up-to-date.

The way BMD solved the problem 'Which product configuration is correct?' in the past is as follows. Before an order could be forwarded to production, it had to be checked for accuracy. Problems like missing options, incompatible or incorrect options had to be identified and corrected. Instructions for production control also needed to be added. This configuration process, referred to as 'order clearing' was done manually by experienced members of BMD's technical marketing staff. Corrective actions were necessary for a considerable percentage of orders.

In some cases, corrections can be made directly by order processing. (For example: A necessary option must be ordered and this option is free of charge.) In other cases, the sales office or the customer has to be asked for a corrected configuration because the factory cannot decide what the customer really needs or wants. (For example: the customer must order exactly one option from a pool of necessary options with costs; or the customer has ordered two incompatible options.)

It turned out that considerable numbers of orders forwarded were still incorrect after manual order clearing. The later an error in an order is detected the more expensive it is to correct it. In the worst case a product which does not fit the customer's needs is manufactured and shipped.

When we decided to build an expert system for the order clearing problem the users defined the objectives shown in Figure 3.3.

* better quality of order processing

* faster than manual process

* knowledge maintenance by end users

* relief of boring routine tasks

Figure 3.3   Requirements for automatic order clearing

Order processing was to be improved by reducing the rate of incorrect orders forwarded and by reducing the amount of 'change orders'. Furthermore, an order clearing system should be permanently available so that order processing becomes independent of vacation and fluctuation among employees. As changes in the underlying order clearing knowledge occur frequently, the knowledge should be maintained by the order clearing experts without the involvement of the EDP department. Finally, the human order clearing experts should be relieved of boring routine tasks. Complex configurations, which used to be cleared in cooperation with sales office or customer, must still be cleared manually.

ORDER CLEARING WITH OCEX

All incoming orders are processed by a central commercial 'Factory Order Processing' system. All order data relevant for order clearing are transmitted to OCEX, and the expert system examines all orders by generating a diagnosis report containing actions recommended for each order.

These actions are processed by an order processing clerk. Correct orders are forwarded directly to production. Incorrect orders which can be changed by the clerk according to the corrective instructions are corrected in the order processing system. Then he forwards these corrected orders to production.

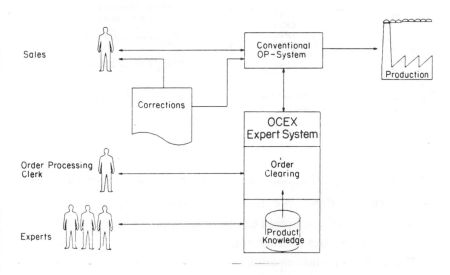

Figure 3.4 The order clearing process using OCEX

The OCEX knowledge base contains the knowledge for order clearing. OCEX offers a user friendly interface, so that end users (production engineers, marketing engineers, order processing clerks) can define and modify order clearing knowledge by themselves.

Example

OCEX receives the following order information for order clearing from the central 'Factory Order Processing System' (Gamm and Herrmann 1988):

— order number and date

— country to which the ordered products are to be shipped

— for each order item:

product number with quantity ordered

options for that product with quantity ordered

```
Order No.: 3847619RE27
Date:    3/1/88
World Country Code: 428        'W-Germany'

Item  Product  Option  Quantity
--------------------------------
  01   HP4711            2
                 #L02    2        'German language'
                 #910    5        'service manual'
                 #K05    1        'dual ECG'
                 #P01    2        'US patient cable'
                 #C01    1        'NIBP'
                 #C03    1        'CO2/NIBP'
                 #N13    1        'PTB/NIBP calibration'
```

Figure 3.5   Order clearing data for a sample order; terms enclosed in quotes are for comment purposes only

Some of the typical option restrictions for medical products are:

— 'Collective' options: an option includes other options

— A maximum of one option can be ordered per product

— An option requires another option

— Two options are incompatible

— A minimum of one option per product is needed.

An order clearing expert who checks the above order would recognize the following order errors:

— As the product is to be shipped to Germany, the German country option #Y72 must be added. The German language option #L02 is included in #Y72, therefore #L02 must be deleted

— A maximum of one free service manual (Option #910) is available per ordered product

— Each dual ECG option #K05 requires a dual temperature option #A04

— US patient cables (Options #P01 to #P05) should only be shipped to the US

— For Germany, one standard option #N13 must be ordered for each ordered option #C01 or #C03.

An instruction for production control must also be added: If the product HP4711 is to be shipped to Germany and the option #K05 is ordered, then the internal language option #107 must be added for each product ordered.

OCEX produces the following diagnosis report for the above sample order. The actions 'ADD>' and 'DEL>' are processed directly by the order processing clerks. They correct the order in the 'Factory Order Processing' system. The action 'CHORDER>' means that the order cannot be changed by the factory, but a change order must be requested from the sales office (#N13 is an option with cost and therefore cannot be added in the factory).

```
-----------------------------------------------------------
Clearing order: 3847619RE27
-----------------------------------------------------------
Item: 01                            Product: HP4711
-----------------------------------------------------------

ADD> #Y72 2

DEL> #L02 2

ADD> #107 2
WRITE> Internal only!

DEL> #910 [3]
WRITE> We can only supply one manual per mainframe.

CHORDER> Dual ECG #K05 requires dual temperature #A05.
         Pls. advise.

CHORDER> Do you really want Patient-Cable-US?
         Pls. advise.

CHORDER> Pls. adjust #N13.
         Qty of #N13 must be 2

-----------------------------------------------------------
```

Figure 3.6 A sample diagnosis report

USE OF RESOURCES

One of the tasks of the 'knowledge-based systems project' team is to support HP entities in the development of expert systems. Support means responsibility for feasibility studies of knowledge-based applications, training of the system analysts involved in AI techniques, helping the selection of appropriate AI tools, and support during design and implementation of the expert system. Our objective is that when the expert system application goes into production, support and enhancements can be done by the cooperating department on their own. Our resources are then freed up for other AI based projects.

Phase ONE   Management Training

Phase TWO   Identify pilot projects

Phase THREE   Training for engineers of cooperating departments

Phase FOUR   Implement project

Phase FIVE   Analyse success of project

Phase SIX   Technology transfer into decentralized business sectors

Figure 3.7 Introduction of knowledge-based technologies at HP GmbH

OCEX was implemented in LISP and Prolog on a HP 9000 workstation. This computer offers a very productive programming environment for the AI programming languages. OCEX runs in interpreted mode. As the average time for clearing one order is only about three seconds it was decided that it is not necessary to compile the application.

The order processing system is running in a commercial computer centre environment on an HP 3000. The order data which are relevant for OCEX are extracted from the order file and transmitted to the HP 9000 by file transfer. The current order processing system will soon be replaced by a next generation order processing system. When the new version of the order processing system is installed, OCEX will generate actions directly for that application so that the orders then are automatically corrected and forwarded to production (automatic order correction).

Course of project

The following overview shows the chronological course of the OCEX project (Gamm and Herrmann 1988).

December 1986:   Implementing a prototype in Prolog

February–   Training of two system analysts from our
June 1987:   EDP department (two days per week each)

July 1987:   System design

August– December 1987:	Implementation
December 1987– January 1988:	Testing, documentation
February– March 1988:	Training of end users Setting up of knowledge for all medical products
April 1988:	OCEX in daily production

KNOWLEDGE BASE MAINTENANCE BY END USERS

The order clearing knowledge consists on the one hand of 'global knowledge', which is relevant and uniform for all medical products. This knowledge does not address a single product, but is dependent on the country into which the product is to be shipped. On the other hand, there is 'product specific knowledge' which is unique for each product. This product specific knowledge describes the configuration for only one product.

```
global facts: table with option
data of 185 countries

------------------------------------

facts and
product-specific           about 50
rules for almost           global
200 products               rules
```

Figure 3.8 OCEX knowledge base

The global knowledge consists of a table containing the country specific requirements for 185 different countries. The corresponding options describe the language, frequency and voltage, cabling, standards and video options. About 50 rules describe the interdependencies of countries and country specific options. As this global knowledge changes very rarely and as the table and the global rules affect all orders, this knowledge is hardcoded. That means the end user cannot change it. If it changes he must ask a knowledge engineer to implement the changes.

The product-specific order clearing knowledge describes the options which can be ordered for the product, the dependencies and restrictions on these options, and instructions for production control purposes. The product-specific knowledge changes 'almost daily'. Some reasons are that one new medical product is released per month on average and that marketing regularly sets up price options which define discounts for specific option combinations and which are valid only for a restricted period of time.

Using a conventional software approach this knowledge would have to be hardcoded in the program. Each time the knowledge changed the users would have to contact the EDP department to implement these changes. This would mean a considerable time delay before knowledge changes could be implemented. The knowledge-based software approach provides the separation of knowledge and control. The major advantage of this separation is that the knowledge can be quickly updated.

OCEX offers a user-friendly interface for end users so that they can define and alter the product-specific knowledge by themselves. The language for expressing this knowledge was designed in cooperation with the end users. The objective was that the entire product specific knowledge can be expressed as simply as possible in that language.

Descriptions for order errors and instructions for production control are expressed by IF–THEN rules. The IF part of a rule defines the conditions for the actions expressed in the THEN part. A condition describes either an order error or a situation in which an internal option for production control purposes has to be added. The actions in the THEN part are the instructions for the order processing clerk. They are printed on the diagnosis report.

In the above order example, five service manuals (option #910) are ordered. There is a restriction for this product that only a maximum of one service manual per product can be ordered. This restriction can be expressed by an IF–THEN rule as follows:

IF the quantity of service manuals (= #910) is greater than
    the quantity of mainframes ordered
THEN delete the superfluous service manuals
    [correct quantity is number of mainframes ordered]
    AND inform the sales office

The end user enters this rule in the OCEX language as follows:

```
IF QTY(#910) > QTY-MAIN
THEN DEL> #910 [QTY-MAIN]
     WRITE> "We can only supply one manual per mainframe."
```

For the diagnosis report OCEX computes how many options must be deleted; in the example above, three service manuals must be deleted (see Figure 3.6).

A more complicated restriction is: Each option #281 requires

— one option #E20
— one option #Z02
— one option #C01 or #C03.

The condition for an order error is:

IF the quantity for ordered #281 is greater than the
  quantity for ordered #E20
OR the quantity for ordered #281 is greater than the
  quantity for ordered #Z02
OR the quantity for ordered #281 is greater than the sum
  of ordered #C01, #C03
THEN request a change order

In OCEX, this restriction can be formulated as follows:

```
IF QTY(#281) > QTY(#E20)
   OR QTY(#281) > QTY(#Z02)
   OR QTY(#281) > SUM(#C01, #C03)
THEN CHORDER> "Each Opt. #281 requires one #E20, one #Z02
              and one #C01 or #C03.
              Please advise."
```

Knowledge of specific products is shared by several people: production engineers, marketing engineers, order processing clerks. We observed that the definition and maintenance of the underlying knowledge is a cooperative and explorative task: when a new complex product is to be released and the order clearing knowledge must be expressed for the expert system, several people sit together and enter the rules into OCEX. Only direct access to OCEX by the end users makes this possible.

The quality and performance of an expert system can only be as good as the knowledge base. As the underlying order clearing knowledge continually changes we introduced some administrative procedures to ensure that knowledge is current, complete and accurate. First, for each product a production engineer was assigned to be responsible for the correctness of the underlying OCEX knowledge. Each production engineer receives a knowledge base report on a regular basis on those products for which he is responsible. Then we introduced a further sign-off procedure within the 'production change order' process. That means no new product or new option for an existing product can be released nor can any existing option be changed unless the appropriate OCEX knowledge is set up. Thus, the introduction of the expert system has led to better control of the entire product design and release process.

REPRESENTATION AND REASONING

Options which can be ordered for a product are stored as Prolog facts. When the user enters a product specific rule, it is checked for syntax, and if correct, compiled into a Prolog rule. All facts and rules about one product are stored in one file.

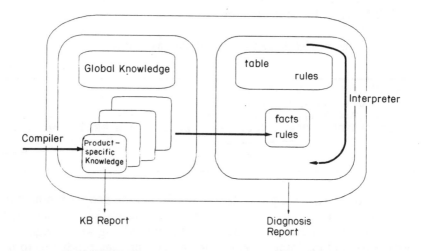

Figure 3.9 OCEX architecture

The global country table and the global rules are loaded permanently. For each order item the necessary product knowledge is loaded (in Prolog terms 'consulted') into working memory. All rules are processed sequentially. Each firing rule produces a piece of text on the diagnosis report, the text being expressed in the THEN part of the rule.

As there are 'item spanning rules' the knowledge of more than one product must be concurrently loaded in the working memory. Item spanning rules describe restrictions for options which concern several products. We implemented a FIFO strategy to keep the knowledge of a maximum of three products concurrently available in working memory.

There are on average 10 rules defined for each product. Very complex products are described by more than 70 rules.

USER INTERFACE

When first designing the user interface for OCEX we planned to use a bit-mapped display to offer a graphically oriented user interface. We asked the users and they wanted a 'very simple, form based user interface similar to those applications they have been using so far and which are available on a character based terminal'.

Therefore, the user interface was designed in cooperation with the experts according to the following design principles:

— simple and uniform interface

— as little text as possible on each screen

— minimal number of user inputs to perform a desired action

— no mouse, but function keys as input devices

— hierarchy of menus and forms

— user input by selecting a menu entry or by filling in a form

— help text for each form and each field

Figure 3.10 shows the screen for maintaining a rule (adding a rule or editing an existing one). The user defines a name and validity period for each product specific rule.

After the rule has been entered it is checked for syntactic and certain semantic errors. If errors are detected a message is printed on the last line. The cursor is positioned at the place where the error has been detected. In the example shown in Figure 3.11 below the #E02 has not been set up as a valid option for the product.

Frequently used patterns for the IF-part or the THEN-part of a rule can be copied into the rule text through the HELP facility (illustrated in Figure 3.12).

No explanation facility was required by the users. In order to support maintenance of the knowlege base by the end users, OCEX offers a module for online order clearing by which the OCEX knowledge can be tested. The expert enters an order, calls 'Order Clearing', and the diagnosis report is printed on screen (see Figure 3.13). The name of the

```
------------------------------------------------------------------
 OCEX                      Maintain Rule
------------------------------------------------------------------

 Product: HP4711      Rule:   EXTBBN-HP4711-DUAL-PRESS-SPECIAL-3

                      Start:  _____    End:
                              YY/MM/DD            YY/MM/DD

 IF      QTY(#281) > QTY(#E20)_____
         OR QTY(#281) > QTY(#Z02)_____
         OR QTY(#281) > SUM(#C01, #C03)_____

         _____
         _____
         _____

 THEN   CHORDER> "Each Opt. #281 requires one #E20, one #Z02__
         _____and one #C01 or #C03._____
         _____Please advise."_____

         _____
         _____
         _____

 ---------------------------------------------------------------
 ---------------------------------------------------------------
```

```
 ┌──────┐┌─────┐┌─────┐┌──────┐┌─────┐┌─────┐  ┌──────┐┌──────┐
 │ENTER ││     ││     ││CLEAR ││     ││     │  │HELP  ││EXIT  │
 │      ││     ││     ││ORDER ││     ││     │  │      ││      │
 └──────┘└─────┘└─────┘└──────┘└─────┘└─────┘  └──────┘└──────┘
```

Figure 3.10   OCEX screen

```
------------------------------------------------------------------
 OCEX                      Maintain Rule
------------------------------------------------------------------

 Product: HP4711      Rule:   EXTBBN-HP4711-DUAL-PRESS-SPECIAL-3

                      Start:  _____    End:
                              YY/MM/DD            YY/MM/DD

 IF      QTY(#281) > QTY(#E02)_____
         OR QTY(#281) > QTY(#Z02)_____  _____
         OR QTY(#281) > SUM(#C01, #C03)_____

         _____
         _____

 THEN   CHORDER> "Each Opt. #281 requires one #E20, one #Z02__
         _____and one #C01 or #C03._____
         _____Please advise."_____

         _____
         _____
         _____

 ---------------------------------------------------------------
 #E02 is not a known option or option set. (2355)
 ---------------------------------------------------------------
```

```
 ┌──────┐┌─────┐┌─────┐┌──────┐┌─────┐┌─────┐  ┌──────┐┌──────┐
 │ENTER ││     ││     ││CLEAR ││     ││     │  │HELP  ││EXIT  │
 │      ││     ││     ││ORDER ││     ││     │  │      ││      │
 └──────┘└─────┘└─────┘└──────┘└─────┘└─────┘  └──────┘└──────┘
```

Figure 3.11   Error message during entry of a rule

```
COUNTRY(........)
COUNTRY(........) AND

QTY(#...) <> QTY-MAIN
QTY(#...) > QTY-MAIN

QTY(#...) <> QTY(#...)
QTY(#...) > QTY(#...)

SUM(.-OPTIONS) <> QTY-MAIN
SUM(#..., #...) <> QTY-MAIN
SUM(.-OPTIONS) > QTY-MAIN
SUM(#..., #...) > QTY-MAIN

QTY(#...) <> SUM(......)
QTY(#...) > SUM(......)
```

Figure 3.12 OCEX help screen: patterns for IF part of a rule

```
------------------------------------------------------------------
Clearing order: 3847619RE27
------------------------------------------------------------------
Item: 01                                         Product: HP4711
------------------------------------------------------------------

     ADD> #Y72 2
     <<< GLOB-RULE-2 >>>


     DEL> #L02 2
     <<< GLOB-RULE-5-3 >>>


     ADD> #107 2
     WRITE> Internal only!
     <<< INTBBN-HP4711-GERMANY-2 >>>


     DEL> #910 [3]
     WRITE> We can only supply one manual per mainframe.
     <<< EXTBBN-HP4711-SERVICE-MANUAL >>>
```

		NEXT PAGE	PREV PAGE			HELP	EXIT

Figure 3.13 A diagnosis report produced during online order clearing: an explanation (= which rule has fired) is printed for each proposed action

rule which fired is written for each proposed action, so the expert can edit the corresponding rule if the action is not correct.

EVALUATION

* in daily use since April '88

* savings in order processing
(direct – $50k per year,
indirect – $300k per year)

* experts are relieved of boring routine duties

* transaction volume reduced by 30%

* orders forwarded now 10 times more accurate

* orders are checked and corrected in a consistent manner

* experts maintain the knowledge base by themselves without the help of programmers

Figure 3.14 Summary of OCEX results

OCEX has been in routine daily use since April 1988. The order clearing batch process takes about 5 to 10 minutes each night, including order data generation and file transfer from the commercial environment to our technical workstation.

We have calculated that with OCEX Hewlett-Packard saves about $350,000 per year. Directly, BMD saves about $50K per year just from the labour saved in reviewing and correcting orders manually. The order clearing experts can now concentrate on the few orders (< 1%) OCEX cannot handle because no correction can be done without direct contact with the sales office or to the customer. This is the case if complex product configurations are needed by the customer.

The original demand for the expert system came from the order clearing clerks because they felt this task was a boring routine duty. Now the expert system has relieved them of that duty.

Indirect savings are more difficult to quantify in dollars. Orders forwarded to production are now 10 times more accurate compared to when they were checked by humans. The increased accuracy of the resulting orders leads to improved material planning for production, reduction in rework at the factory and reduction of production change orders. We estimate all these indirect savings come to about $300K a year.

ORGANIZATIONAL ISSUES

When Hewlett-Packard Germany decided to invest in expert systems, it was also decided to choose a top-down approach for the introduction of this technology. That means: first convince management, then look for promising pilot applications. The section 'Knowledge-Based Systems Project' was funded with the objective of defining projects with partners in that new technology. We believe that commitment of top management is the key to a successful introduction and distribution of such new technologies.

* restricted domain

* knowledge already exists

* static knowledge structure

* ROI

* problem difficult/impossible to solve conventionally

* 'intelligent assistant'

* motivation with end users

Figure 3.15 Selection criteria for pilot expert systems projects

We had some brainstorming sessions with R & D Managers, Manufacturing Managers, and Project Managers to select candidates for expert system projects. Many of them proposed problems for which projects were already defined but had failed; for which only a poor or partly manual solution exists; or for which the requirements were so complex and 'galactic' that the problem was not even properly understood. One reason is that the area of Artificial Intelligence sometimes creates unrealistic expectations of what can be solved with the underlying techniques. Therefore we demanded a restricted problem domain.

We wanted to start with problems for which the knowledge for solving them already exists. That means the problem has up to now been solved by human experts. It was not our goal to first acquire knowledge, but we wanted to represent knowledge already existing in the heads of people, written in procedures, and applied by humans.

In many problem domains the knowledge changes very rapidly. Typically, knowledge engineers acquire the knowledge from the human experts and construct the knowledge base. When the knowledge changes, the user contacts the knowledge engineer who then implements the changes (Prerau 1987). For our pilot expert system projects, we require that at least the structure of the knowledge be static. The contents will change, however. In this case, the knowledge can be formulated by a higher level formal language. This language can be used as a basis for building a compiler which can transform the knowledge expressed in that language into an internal representation (AI language or shell). An interface for knowledge base maintenance can be offered to end users.

One of the most important criteria is to have selected a project with high ROI, which means money can be saved with the planned application. A new technology can only gain wide acceptance within a commercial environment if it saves money!

An additional important selection criterion is to choose a problem which can only be solved using that new technology or which can only be solved very awkwardly and inefficiently using conventional software technologies. As there is a considerable amount of investment (training, new procedures) necessary to introduce new technologies, these technologies must provide advantages and savings.

Humans take several years to become experts. Today and also in the next decades, no expert systems can be built which will be able to substitute for the entire, enormous expertise of humans. It is possible to represent and code a part of the knowledge of experts in order to solve some of their routine tasks.

In order to obtain the knowledge of an expert we need a considerable amount of his time. Also, only experts can verify and judge the problem solving quality of expert systems. If the expert system takes over some of his routine duties there are normally no cooperation problems (Herrmann 1987).

LESSONS LEARNT

Typical successful commercial applications are found within the areas of data interpretation, configuration, planning/simulation, and monitoring (Waterman 1986). We believe that the knowledge-based programming approach leads to a new quality of software development for such problems.

* Prototyping

* Productive environment for software development

* Active User participation during implementation

* Set up knowledge = interactive explorative process

* End users can maintain their knowledge

Figure 3.16 A new quality for software development

During the whole design and construction phase of OCEX the cooperation of the users was very productive and enthusiastic. When OCEX went into production I asked them why they were so convinced that OCEX would be a success. Their answer: 'You wrote a prototype within only three weeks. When we saw what is possible with that new expert system technology we were convinced that this approach will solve our problems!'. We learnt that an early prototype supports the involvement and cooperation of the end users.

We had the experience that the users cannot specify in advance all the system features they need. The building of OCEX was done in several loops of 'design, implementation, end user evaluation'. The productive development environment for LISP and Prolog on the workstation supported the repeated changes and reimplementations. Also, the experts were not able to enter at once all details of the order clearing knowledge, but they needed some time until the entire knowledge became stable and complete. The knowledge base maintenance module of OCEX makes this explorative process easier.

If we were doing OCEX again we would investigate a redesign of the OCEX user interface. We believe that requirements of users have changed

* Conversion of research results into applications

* Goals of business management become more important

* Hybrid approaches influence future developments (solutions, hardware)

* More realistic expectations

Figure 3.17: Trends for knowledge-based systems

because office software with window based, object-oriented, and graphic interfaces are more widespread and therefore more acceptable.

CONCLUSIONS

We expect the trends for knowledge-based systems to be as shown in Figure 3.17.

The main advantages of the knowledge-based programming approach for the order clearing problem can be summarized as follows:

1. The underlying knowledge changes almost daily. The knowledge base can only be kept up-to-date by the experts through direct and immediate access to the knowledge.

2. Knowledge maintenance for our products is a highly interactive and explorative process. Knowledge for complex products is set up together and interactively by several different experts.

3. The separation of knowledge and control makes it possible to design and build an interface for end users so that they can maintain the knowledge by themselves.

4. The separation of knowledge and control enables a simple and efficient geographical distribution of product knowledge.

REFERENCES

Gamm, W. and Herrmann, F. (1988). OCEX—Ein Expertensystem zur Überprüfung von Kundenaufträgen und zur Konfigurierung von Produktionssteuerungsanforderungen. In K.-P. Fähnrich (ed.): *Expertensysteme in Planung und Produktion*, Kongreßband, KOMMTECH '88.

Herrmann, F. (1987). OCEX—Ein Expertensystem zur Konfiguration von Kundenaufträgen. In H. Wildemann (ed.) *Expertensysteme in der Produktion*, *Tagungsbericht, Gesellschaft für Management und Technologie, 1987*.

Holsapple, C.W. *et al* (1987). Expert System Integration. In B.G. Silverman (ed.) *Expert Systems for Business*, Addison Wesley, Reading, MA.

Mertens, P. (1987). Expertensysteme in den betrieblichen Funktionsbereichen— Chancen, Erfolge, Mißerfolge. In W. Brauer and W. Wahlster (eds) *Wissensbasierte Systeme, 2. Int. GI-Kongreß München 1987*, Springer Berlin.

Prerau, D. (1987). Knowledge Acquisition in Expert System Development. *AI Magazine*, 8, No. 2.

Waterman, D. A. (1986). *A Guide to Expert Systems*, Addison Wesley, London.

4

Tracker—Lessons from a First Expert System

Chas Church

ABSTRACT

The author was jointly responsible for TRACKER, an expert system for electronics diagnosis and repair. The TRACKER project resulted in both a specific expert system and a Prolog-based shell later to be used for a range of diagnostic applications. The work was commenced in mid 1983 and this paper both outlines the early work and shows how the lessons learnt from and since the TRACKER project have been effectively used by the author in subsequent expert systems projects.

INTRODUCTION

The first version of TRACKER was the joint work of the author and Dr George Pollard (now with Expertech Ltd) and was undertaken when both originators were with British Telecom. Based on our initial innovation, the TRACKER shell has undergone considerable further development (including a major reimplementation for which the author had early design responsibility) and remains successfully in use within British Telecom.

The original TRACKER expert system, although having fully separate shell and knowledge base, was designed to support the specific task of diagnosis and repair of faults on a particular model of a complex switched-mode power unit. Following this successful initial application the shell was both enhanced and generalized so that it could be used for applications covering a wider range of electronics diagnostic and related problems.

Although much of the TRACKER experience is still relevant and useful, there have been considerable expert systems advances in the intervening years. The author's own practices have also changed for reasons of efficiency, to support a wider range of applications and to respond to an increasing need for expert systems to answer commercial rather than research challenges.

For these reasons, this paper complements the author's personal recollections of the early TRACKER project with a commentary based on some of the lessons learnt both from it and from subsequent project work. This commentary shows how the experiences provided by the TRACKER work have been applied, but in many cases revised or radically extended, to expert systems implementations for which he has since been responsible.

The TRACKER project is described under topic headings in the approximate order that issues might be considered in a present day project. To clarify the contrast between early and current experience and practice, the word 'Update' is used as a preface to section paragraphs dealing with revised or later ideas and practices.

OBJECTIVES

The TRACKER work was motivated by three principal objectives. First, the originators wished to prove to themselves that they were capable of building a commercially worthwhile expert system. Second, and a particularly strong objective of George Pollard, was the desire to demonstrate the utility and appropriateness of Prolog as the basis of an expert system shell. Third, was the wish to provide an exemplar of expert systems usefulness to British Telecom management.

The first two objectives were personal, only marginally related to the needs of British Telecom, but provided the essential motivation to the work. The third objective, although providing us with the necessary public justification for our activities, was the weakest real objective and was primarily seen as a means of obtaining formal authorization for us to undertake development work in the expert systems area.

In the event the construction of TRACKER satisfied all three objectives admirably. As a result of TRACKER we learnt the groundwork of our trade in terms of practical knowledge acquisition and representation and in the design of inference engines and useful user interfaces. George Pollard did able and very clever service on behalf of micro-Prolog (defeating its natural inclinations where necessary) to produce an elegant, user-friendly shell within the most limited confines of CP/M running on an 8-bit microcomputer. He inevitably took some of his acquired skills forward into the successful commercial development of Xi Plus and, latterly, into the design of the inference engine of the C-based versions of the same product.

We demonstrated the potential worth of expert systems technology to British Telecom senior management and so satisfied that objective in the short term by being established as a formal group to develop engineering expert systems. In the longer term, and in common with many other major corporates, British Telecom appears to remain in the 'proving' stage and is still making only marginal use of expert systems. There is still much to be achieved within a knowledge-based industry perhaps more rich in opportunity than any other.

Update

In current projects, especially where these are the first within a particular company, there remains a need to prove the utility of the technology. However, the proof is not now whether an expert system can actually be built (this now being widely accepted) but whether the resultant system can provide worthwhile business benefit. In most respects current objectives must initially correspond to the third TRACKER objective. Personal objectives and the desire to pursue technical convictions (as in our case with Prolog) cannot be prime project motivators unless workers are either research funded or prepared to work in their own time.

When a company has completed an initial system, and has satisfied itself both to the viability and usefulness of the technology, then objectives must be assembled in precisely the same way as any other IT project. Moreover, even if a degree of indulgence has been allowed in an initial project, proposed further expert systems implementations must compete with conventional implementation routes. TRACKER would undoubtedly have run faster in BASIC than Prolog and, if further examples of 'fully-compiled' expertise had come along, the conventional route may have taken precedence.

APPROVAL AND FUNDING

TRACKER was an example of 'technology push' and was illegitimately conceived by two enthusiastic strangers who met on a train. George Pollard and I connived to find a first-rate task and an articulate expert within British Telecom, worked at home under our own steam and did not let the thought of budgets or formal project authorization even cross our minds. It was perhaps just good fortune that the initial system proved to be so successful. As a result we were legitimized and given *post hoc* respectability and budgets to generalize the shell, recruit further staff and undertake additional diagnostic systems and wider AI projects.

A 'champion' was vitally important to our metamorphosis and continued existence. We were well served in this respect and it remains vitally necessary for all new initiatives to be protected from scrutiny during the period that teams are assembled and first-attempt systems are built.

Update

TRACKER was primarily motivated by personal interests and enthusiasm. For better or worse, enthusiasm is not now a sole sufficient condition for starting an expert systems project. Apart from the requirements to prove technical feasibility and utility almost before a project gets underway, there is now the most rigorous need to undertake a cost–benefit analysis in respect of the promised business benefits which the final delivery system will satisfy.

Much to the detriment of expert systems credibility, many early projects saw the delivery of a prototype almost as a badge of success. The fact that successful construction of a prototype is just one indicator that a full system may be feasible and useful was often forgotten in the ensuing self-satisfaction. These days the term 'prototype' is becoming of decreasing relevance. In many cases, experience makes it now possible to fully predetermine and design the general structure of a proposed system. The experimental prototype is often no longer necessary. However, in a change of emphasis, a pilot system, illustrating breadth, depth and functionality of the final product may be required for marketing or funding purposes.

Thus, for project approval and budgetary purposes, the project sponsor not only has an early specification against which he can checklist eventual system deliverables but has also a good estimate of both pilot and full delivery system costs. He will also expect to be presented with a convincing appraisal of the anticipated benefits, both quantitative and qualitative, which will result from the system's use. In an initial development the benefits may legitimately include the establishment of an expert systems capability within the firm.

As a result sponsors of current expert systems projects are able (and should now expect) to compare quantified benefits with anticipated development and delivery cost of the system. Enthusiasm remains an essential requirement for expert systems development but is now not solely sufficient for a project to proceed.

SYSTEMS SPECIFICATION

Although late and current versions of TRACKER were well specified, there was no specification of the initial version. In fact, the concept of a 'specification' for an expert system would have been considered either an unknown concept or a contradiction in terms by many of the reigning expert systems gurus of the day.

In actuality, although a formal specification document was not produced, the scope and functionality of the system were precisely defined by the requirements of the task to be supported and the environment where that support was to be delivered. Our objective was to represent all acquirable knowledge from the expert diagnostician and to advise on and explain to users all the various diagnoses in his repertoire. Since our expert was very experienced in his diagnosis and repair work, and was also immensely cooperative and articulate, we were well able to satisfy our implicit specification.

Similarly, it was our intention to support not only the end result but also the particularly efficient style of diagnosis of our expert. We recognized several different inference methods and informally specified and clarified these in our discussions.

Many diagnostic tasks can be undertaken by exhaustive search. The real skill and experience of the expert diagnostician rests in his ability to recognize early combinations of symptoms and to take short cuts in his search. In some cases TRACKER was required to undertake a procedural search, perhaps checking out a suspected chain of components until the faulty one was discovered. In other cases, where a fault on a particular component was hypothesized, various confirmatory tests were undertaken to prove the fault without actually unsoldering the component and perhaps causing further damage. Each of these different activities required the implementation of appropriate control structures in the shell and, although not embraced in a formal specification document, they were well identified and understood as functional requirements.

In respect of the knowledge within the system (as distinct from specification of the functionality of the shell), there was never any separate specification except that of the knowledge base itself. In retrospect, the global specification that the system would entirely replicate the expert's knowledge in respect of the power unit was somewhat ambitious.

Update

Specification is now a necessary and sensible part of any expert system development. In conventional software development the specification is produced 'up front' and is directly related to a statement of user requirements. The specification is used both as the starting point for systems design and, later on, for checking whether the eventually delivered system matches the user (and contractual) requirements.

Similarly, much of an expert system can, and should, now be specified at the outset of a development project. Leaving aside for the moment the question of specification of the knowledge within the system, there is usually no excuse not to specify the hardware and software to be used, the nature of the user and maintenance interfaces, the requirements for conventional program and existing database integration and the expectations for response times and system performance. Such latter matters can be of crucial importance, particularly for multi-user mainframe systems, and early specification is imperative.

Pre-implementation specification of the knowledge to be encoded within an expert system seems, at first sight, to be something of a nonsense. How is it possible to specify that which is still to be discovered? However, there has to be something better than our TRACKER promise (to ourselves) to acquire and encode all of the diagnostician's relevant knowledge. If we cannot measure the scope and complexity of the knowledge then how, in advance, can we promise a feasible implementation? More important, how can we estimate the cost of the work involved in transferring the knowledge to a working expert system? In TRACKER the essential challenge was to see if we could acquire and encode whatever knowledge was there, and, as previously stated, budgets and estimates were irrelevant.

In the intervening period since TRACKER it has become far easier to specify knowledge to be encoded and this is now a regular part of any costed proposition for an expert system. Most specifications depend on a scoping interview with the expert followed by the preparation of an agreed specification with the project sponsor. It is not particularly difficult to provide a relatively unambiguous description of the expertise (and exceptions to it) which has to be represented and to cost the knowledge engineering effort accordingly. Difficulties, where they remain, are largely in the areas of depth to be covered and user groups to be supported.

In TRACKER we covered within the system some cases based on a single instance reported by the expert. In other words, we laboriously encoded diagnostic routines to isolate a particular component which had only caused a problem once in the expert's several years of experience. Such thoroughness is very creditable but, in economic terms, does not always make sense. Most expert systems must have a 'cut-off' point where the existing expert knowledge is exhausted and the system must be handed back gracefully to human control for a novel solution.

In economic terms the cut-off point may be related to the population of known cases to be supported. For instance, in a pensions scheme advisory expert system, one may choose not to encode the means of allowing for service in the armed forces prior to World War II even though a few old soldiers still remain in employment. In such cases the system specification must make it clear which cases are to be covered or, alternatively, must state some agreed means of deciding individual coverage issues.

Similarly, any specification must clearly state the user group(s) which the system will support. In TRACKER we blindly envisaged an archetypal experienced technician who would use the system. This could have proved fatal in a tightly costed system where some 40 per cent of the effort can be expended in implementing the user interface. It has been my own post-TRACKER experience to create systems which address the needs of the assumed user group only to find that a subsidiary, usually junior, user group is required to use the system. The effort involved in providing a user interface to support this junior group, with all the consequent extra help and explanation needed, has almost doubled the effort required to complete the implementation. Thus specification of the anticipated user profile is essential for any commercially implemented system.

The scoping work required to develop a knowledge base specification is, of course, not wasted as it is easily incorporated in the effort that would in any case be expended on knowledge acquisition. However, completing the scoping in advance has a further valuable contribution in respect of cost–benefit analysis.

The scoping interview, if properly carried out, will highlight the proportion of cases, at any detailed stage of a problem solving exercise, that can be supported by the expert system. Normally this will be well in excess of 80 per cent for most problem stages. On the basis of estimates for the various percentages of cases and sub-cases that can be covered (and the corresponding residual cases that will require to remain in the hands of the existing human experts), it is possible to work out reasonably precisely the overall manpower savings resulting from use of the system. Set against such figures will be the costs of providing and staffing the system.

It can thus easily be seen that the knowledge scoping and specification effort, in addition to providing a good understanding between sponsor and implementor, can also provide both the overall costs and the required cost-justification for the system. For the expense of a half-day session with an expert (and it usually takes little more), plus a little analysis, the results are clearly worthwhile.

SYSTEM DESIGN

The design of TRACKER, like its specification, followed an iterative prototyping process. For this reason the design was part of the development process rather than a precursor to it. In retrospect the process seems reasonable since we had few models and no previous experience to work upon. In the long term there was a penalty to be paid in that we were obliged to subject TRACKER to a complete redesign and reimplementation. This was not really due to limitations in the existing shell but, as in many examples of conventional software, the burden of modification became more and more difficult as increasing functionality was required. Following the third application using the original shell we decided to take in all the modifications by way of a complete redesign and it is the reimplemented system that remains in successful use.

Update

In current projects it is my practice to attempt a fairly detailed system design relatively soon after the initial scoping knowledge acquisition. This is necessary both for feasibility and cost–benefit analysis purposes.

However, the facility to produce such a design rests on the experience of a series of expert systems implementations and the current availability of adequate shells. With TRACKER we had neither the experience nor the shell and had to design and develop both as we went along. Moreover, even with current systems, the detailed design has often to be radically modified as the development proceeds even though the overall structure and system size and consequent development time and cost seem to remain largely as initially envisaged.

EVALUATION CRITERIA AND METHODS

Evaluation criteria were not formally set up at the start of the TRACKER project but, again, were implicit in our project planning. Apart from our own assessment in terms of our personal objectives, we both believed that TRACKER would be primarily assessed as evidence that AI and Logic Programming could be of commercial benefit to British Telecom. Thus we assumed that TRACKER would be primarily evaluated as a powerful expert systems exemplar. Its assessment in respect of a specific requirement to support less experienced diagnosticians was always and, in the event, correctly assumed to be of secondary assessment importance.

Update

Evaluation and assessment are now well established elements of any good expert system project design. Some evaluation criteria may be directly related to the systems specification and set in terms both of functionality and of breadth of cases to be covered and the depth to which cases may be fully exercised.

Proper user assessment is now regarded as vitally important. As part of the evaluation process, it is now designed as an ongoing activity to be undertaken during system implementation rather than something to leave to the end of the project. The selection and commitment of user assessment panels and their management by an assessor independent of the implementation team is seen as a major contribution to a successful expert systems project.

Thorough user assessment arrangements have a major effect on the confidence of the project team as well as a significant effect on the minimization of costs of the overall project. Put simply, ongoing user assessment means that errors and misunderstandings are detected early when they are cheap to correct rather than by radical revision at the tail-end of the implementation.

HARDWARE AND SOFTWARE RESOURCES

TRACKER was initially implemented using micro-Prolog running under CP/M on an 8-bit CASU microcomputer. The software selection was made on the basis of our commitment to demonstrate the utility of Prolog. We chose micro-Prolog because the Prolog implementations from Logic Programming Associates were, and arguably still are, the most advanced of their kind. The hardware selection was made so as to conform with the delivery requirement to run the system on CASU microcomputers already available at British Telecom's local repair workshops.

At the time that TRACKER was conceived there were few if any readily available PC shells and, even if they had been available, we had no authorized funds available to purchase them. In the event, the later versions of the TRACKER shell have recently been described as having far greater utility and suitablity for their purpose than any of the currently commercially available shells. It must be remembered that the TRACKER shell was dedicated to a particular form of application, that of benchtop electronics diagnosis, whereas for commercial reasons most current shells are generalist in design. A powerful lesson from TRACKER is in the power of domain-dedicated (or inclination) shells to support particular classes of expert activity.

Nevertheless, had we been contemplating the TRACKER project today, we would undoubtedly have used a commercial shell for the purpose and either accepted or overcome (i.e. by bespoke extensions) its generalist limitations. The result would undoubtedly have been less powerful but the system would have been built with far less effort.

Update

Although the actual choice would undoubtedly be different, the basis on which we chose the TRACKER hardware would undoubtedly be the same. In most of my own intervening and current work it has always been my objective to deliver a 'hardware cost-free' expert system. Thus it is wherever possible my intention to provide the delivery expert system within the user's already existing hardware environment. The exceptions to this rule, inevitably resulting in an implementation on an AI workstation, are where either the complexity of the application, the needs of the user interface (in terms of bandwidth etc) or the extent of the financial leverage of the resultant system (e.g. in international tax etc) justify the special purchase of hardware to support the delivery system.

INTEGRATION

Like most early expert systems, TRACKER was a stand-alone system not integrated with other software or databases. This was not a limitation since a separate database of fault-prone components was already in existence and it was a relatively trivial matter to exit TRACKER to update this database after a successful session using the system. Similarly, TRACKER was used at remote workshop sites not networked or with access to corporate mainframes. More by luck than design we had chosen an application where successful usage did not demand the extra effort resulting from a need to integrate.

Update

Perhaps one of the key turning points in the commercial acceptance of expert systems is their transition from isolated advisors to systems fully integrated with existing software. It is interesting to note that, only until recently, integration has either been impossible or very awkward.

The need for integration in many cases underlines the requirement to deliver within an existing hardware environment. In my work since TRACKER the ability to call upon existing data and to interface with established conventional programs has often been the key reason for which project approval has been granted. On the other hand, especially where 'unfriendly' hardware has been involved, the integration work has often overshadowed the expert systems implementation in terms of both difficulty and time.

Current systems depend on their ability to call upon databases, invoke decision support systems or offer seamless integration with conventional mainframe software.

STAFF RECRUITMENT AND TRAINING

George Pollard and I recruited ourselves as the ideal candidates for the task of implementing the first TRACKER system. We complemented our academic experience with 'on the job' training and learnt some of each other's skills. This meant that George Pollard became rather proficient at talking to experts and unravelling how they think. For my part, I learnt a little of the more curious aspects of Prolog.

For the second phase of the TRACKER work, following our 'legitimization', we recruited primarily on the basis of enthusiasm and application. Major expert systems implementations are achieved more by sweat than genius (there are those who say this is proven conclusively by my own experience) and we chose bright hard workers to join us.

Update

Staff recruitment and training is now much better organized and it is unlikely that either of the subversive TRACKER originators would be deemed suitable. AI/Expert Systems degree and other courses are now readily available and there is now a steady supply of first-rate candidates from which to recruit implementation teams. Where it is not possible to recruit dedicated staff for a complete implementation team, it is now common to mount Technology Transfer Programmes so that, for instance, existing DP staff can take an increasing role in a project and, in due course, cope with the ongoing maintenance requirement. Most of my post-TRACKER work has involved the secondment of trainees and the experience has proved beneficial for all concerned.

DEVELOPMENT AND DELIVERY ENVIRONMENTS

TRACKER was both developed and delivered on the same machine. There was really no other choice available to us particularly since we were determined to use micro-Prolog and this was then only available under CP/M. Many of the problems of space and screen management would have had to be faced twice if a development environment had been available. In retrospect, its absence was no hardship.

Update

In the main, development within the intended delivery environment is still our general practice and avoids many of the complications (or impossibilities) of porting an application from development to delivery environment. Nevertheless, and for a widening range of applications, the promise of developing within a powerful workstation environment and then delivering on a cost-effective run-time environment is becoming a reality.

Similarly, the availability of powerful development tools on comparatively mundane hardware is softening the line between prototyping and run-time environments. In current work, where a separate development environment has been employed, it is our practice to provide a knowledge base maintenance system (essentially a dedicated maintenance tool) within the delivery system. Such a maintenance system requires neither the full functionality nor performance of the primary development tool but enables the regular updating of the delivery system without the need to purchase or support a full prototyping environment.

USER INVOLVEMENT

We did not bother to involve users for the main part of the TRACKER implementation. It was obvious to us that, once finished, they would fall over themselves to use our masterpiece. We were fully convinced that there was an eager multitude of technicians waiting silently for us to provide a solution to the mystery of the broken power unit. We were also quite sure that we knew best about how to deliver the expert's knowledge.

In the event we did find a user and he was kind. From him, and from the many others who followed him we learnt two important lessons. First, a well designed expert system provided to support a specific task (e.g. a specific manufacturer's type and model of switched-mode power unit) can impart sufficient generalist knowledge for the user to become able to repair a whole range of similar equipment (e.g. power units of different design but similar principles from various other manufacturers).

Second, and after spending hours of effort and ingenuity to produce the 'mandatory' expert systems help screens and trace facilities, we found that our users hardly ever used them. They knew that the facilities were there but hardly ever bothered to push the F1 key. They just wanted to mend as many power units as possible.

Update

Here there has been a radical change since TRACKER and it is now my practice not only to involve users in system assessment on an ongoing basis but also to undertake specific 'user knowledge acquisition'.

With TRACKER we had no idea of the shape of the void which we were to fill in our users' minds. It was by good fortune, and by the lucky choice of a good expert, that the acquired knowledge met the delivery requirement. In current projects it is not unusual to spend up to one third of the knowledge acquisition effort on acquiring user requirements, particularly in terms of the style and format of the knowledge to be presented to them. Experts and novices order and view their knowledge (or lack of it) in different ways and the successful expert system, like the good teacher, will deliver its content in the way best suited to the novice.

The fact that TRACKER taught us that users generalize from domain-specific expert systems has also not been forgotten and it is my practice always to attempt to design systems which impart some elements of training in respect of the general principles involved. One day there will be a proper integration between the CBT and expert systems disciplines to the general betterment of both. In the meantime the expert systems training side effects cannot be ignored and must be utilized to best advantage.

KNOWLEDGE ACQUISITION

Prior to commencing work on TRACKER, the author had extensively read and had had some practical experience of the 'proper' methods of knowledge acquisition. Even in advance of going to the repair workshop where he was to acquire the knowledge for the first TRACKER system, he was aware that card sorting and the like might be greeted with polite Northern derision. Therefore, not having the nerve to do things properly, he read up the few manuals and circuit diagrams that were available for the power unit, bought a new battery for his little tape recorder and set out to talk with the expert.

As a result most of the knowledge for the quite extensive TRACKER expert system came across in the first session of less than a working day. The shoddy practice seemed to work and, although if pressed, he can assemble a somewhat dubious 'scientific' rationale for what he does, he still very efficiently acquires wide and diverse knowledge by the seat of his pants. This does not seem unreasonable since knowledge acquisition is something that we all do every day, whether we are asking road directions, how to fix a shower, or what to do with a defective radio transmitter or accountant, our inbuilt interrogation techniques are probably rather better than the artificial ones that we contrive.

As with most tasks, there was more than one expert available for the first TRACKER implementation. From that first project until now, it has always been my practice to interrogate the experts in isolation rather than listen to their conflict. In many cases equally competent experts will undertake their tasks in completely different structural fashions. The setting of one against another, particularly on a 'line by line' basis is usually quite destructive. It is usually far better to acquire their separate sets of knowledge and, wherever possible, later construct a composite system based on the best elements of each expert's experience.

Although we were novices with an unproven technology, we had no difficulty in getting the cooperation of our primary expert and winning his knowledge. Most truly competent folk will tell you what they know without hesitation. They are well aware that they have the capacity to create new knowledge even if you do manage to encode that which they have given to you. Our expert for TRACKER, and without exception all those who have followed him, seemed to enjoy the knowledge acquisition process as a preferable alternative to work. In his case, and in the case of many of those who have followed, it was the first time that anybody had really cared to know what he knew.

The early TRACKER tapes were transcribed in full with the exception of civilities and comments on food, lavatories and the like. In traditional style each speaker (apart from interjection comments) was identified at the beginning of separate numbered paragraphs.

Update

Although core knowledge acquisition is often best conducted on a conversational basis (as with the early TRACKER systems), the latter stages of an implementation will often use a running partial system as a 'prompt' to tease out the remnants of the expert's knowledge. Styles vary but our own preference is not to enhance the system on-line but to record the comments for subsequent updating of the knowledge base. This is both economical on expert time and avoids the possibility of poor code written under pressure in the expert's presence. Nevertheless, for both core knowledge and enhancements, the use of full transcripts is solely reserved for very difficult areas of the knowledge where the cost and time involved can be reasonably justified.

Thus there has been some considerable change since the TRACKER work and the productive expert system implementor will use an eclectic range of knowledge acquisition techniques, dependent both on the stage of the implementation and the nature of the task to be supported. Nevertheless, the determined interrogator will long prefer to use his lights, tape and video recorders. In such circumstances it is amazing how long he has survived without a Repertory Grid.

INTERMEDIATE REPRESENTATIONS

The term 'intermediate representation' came to our attention some considerable time after the TRACKER work commenced but, in retrospect, it is clear that our objective was to turn the raw transcript into a series of intermediate representations. The stages which we followed were fairly simple and obvious and, although a little time-consuming, are probably still best for the beginner to follow.

The raw transcripts were annotated with ample yellow highlighter (the only colour then available), red pen and margin notes. Key words and phrases, 'topic headings', 'verbatim rules', procedures and 'help text' are just some of the items which are easily identified on this first pass analysis.

The annotated transcript was then used to prepare a 'transcript digest', listing the areas covered at each stage of the dialogue. Typically, a session with an expert lasting for the core part of a working day would result in between fifty and one hundred A4 transcript pages. The resulting digest might be three to five pages long with many of the 'index lines' consisting of just one or two words.

The transcript digest becomes the master index to the source transcript. The transcript itself is converted to intermediate representations in the form of lists, hierarchies, procedural fragments and all the various other artefacts upon which we found it convenient to hang the acquired knowledge. It is to be particularly noted that such intermediate representations are essentially in parallel and are often orthogonal representations of the same knowledge. In this respect most of their content is not truly 'intermediate' (i.e. between the raw knowledge and the code) but is made up of ancilliary representations whose main purpose is to act as a prop to the knowledge engineer's growing understanding of the acquired knowledge.

Although there may be several (mostly redundant) parallel representations, it is very unusual for there to be more than one or two serial intermediate representations since multiple conversions are both unnecessary and lead to error.

The master intermediate representation for TRACKER was based on an A4 photocopied form. This form contained a series of fields/slots and multiple copies of it were completed, each of which had a one-to-one relationship with a final TRACKER system screen. This particular form of representation was very useful for the TRACKER project for reasons which will be described later.

Update

As with the decline in the production of transcripts, efficiency has forced the abandonment of the more superfluous intermediate representations. TRACKER was produced in parallel to the analysis of the knowledge but currently the explicit representations made available by ready-made shells allow the intermediate representation and target knowledge base to largely coalesce. In more than one case we have used the knowledge base appropriate to one shell to be the intermediate representation for another. Such things are encouraging and promise increasing productivity in system implementation.

In TRACKER, apart from some crude 'spidergrams', we hardly used any graphical intermediate representations. The use of powerful graphical environments close-coupled to developing knowledge bases has dramatically changed matters in this respect. The knowledge engineer may now maintain the best overall understanding of the complete system even when engrossed in detail.

REPRESENTATION AND REASONING

We soon discovered a convenient high-level understanding for the knowledge we were to encode in TRACKER. The knowledge of the efficient electronics diagnostician experienced in the faults of a particular piece of equipment embodies a dynamically optimized search routine. This will lead to the aberrant component(s) in the minimum time and with the minimum disruption. Thus the knowledge is primarily procedural where each level of procedure is optimized to show up test irregularities in the shortest time and with the least amount of physical intervention (e.g. unsoldering etc).

Once a test irregularity is found (e.g. an abnormal voltage or oscilloscope signature), the search procedure is dynamically adapted on the basis of this clue to most efficiently close in on the next irregular test indicator. This process continues until a final procedure indicates the precise location of the faulty component(s). This is then verified, usually by direct substitution. Most benchtop diagnosis seems to follow this pattern and, once the 'ethic' is understood, it is one of the easiest to build into an expert system. Again, we were lucky in our choice of task for TRACKER since other tasks are rather harder to understand and represent.

Prolog is ideal to represent the goal structures for conventional diagnostic search. Nevertheless, it required some considerable skill to combine its inherent backward chaining with forward-chaining rules which fired when an aberrant test result occurred. I am sure that the TRACKER project would not have succeeded if George Pollard's exceptional skill with Prolog had not been available. The inference engine was designed in parallel to the knowledge acquisition and analysis and, in the main, was the result of my verbal description to him of the various inference methods employed by the expert. As our knowledge of the expert's diagnostic strategies increased so did the sophistication of the shell needed to support their simulation.

As described above, knowledge acquisition and subsequent analysis resulted in a paper master intermediate representation. Each A4 sheet contained on it the dialogue for a particular screen including questions to be asked, the menu of alternative responses and the coded consequences of each response. The text of associated help screens was also included in a field on the sheets together with those rules which might fire as a result of a particular response to the screen.

The localization of rules to service particular areas of the diagnostic dialogue seemed natural. It is only more latterly that knowledge base segmentation has emphasized the sense of this idea as a support for proper control of inference and run-time efficiency. In the case of TRACKER, although the rules were held locally to the associated text in the paper intermediate representation, they were later combined into a more global knowledge base when coded.

Other intermediate representation sheets contained rules which were not associated with any particular screen. In the main these were to deal with odd groups of symptoms which might be 'noticed' at any stage of the diagnosis and which would immediately change the focus of search to 'home in' on a particular area of the circuit.

Although perhaps rather unusual, and certainly not a form of intermediate representation which I have used since, the TRACKER intermediate representation was both useful and effective. Perhaps the circumstances of the TRACKER collaboration, which will be highlighted next, made it the most suitable for our purposes.

It is worth remembering that George Pollard and I were collaborators at a distance. Our activity was not official and we worked largely in our spare time. As a result there was a requirement to transfer the content of the acquired knowledge, both in terms of the knowledge itself and the inference which supported it, from myself (primarily at the acquisition/analysis stage) to George Pollard (primarily at the shell design and knowledge encoding stage).

The discipline imposed by our separation led to the fact that the design specification of the inference engine was not written down but developed between us largely on the telephone and in occasional face-to-face meetings. The content of the knowledge, on the A4 sheets, was passed between us by post. It is interesting to consider that we did not find an effective way of abstractly describing and transmitting the required inference mechanisms but, at the first attempt, managed to design a simple A4 form which could act as a regular and apparently complete medium for the transmission of the knowledge.

Although our pre-TRACKER training had led us to believe that we would require to come to terms with uncertainty (and TRACKER initially had provision to do this) we were surprised that probabilities and the like did not appear in the knowledge. Perhaps probabilities sometimes lie in the eye of the beholder (CF 97.3%).

TRACKER was of the order of some 200 rules in its first version. This was as nothing compared with later systems but was sufficient for TRACKER to effectively cover its domain. Even in the first version there were generic rules capable of re-use under different circumstances and it is likely that encoding with some of the popular shells available today would have resulted in a larger rule base. There is as yet no proper unit to describe knowledge in quantitative terms and the use of numbers of rules to indicate the size of a system becomes less and less relevant.

Update

TRACKER was primarily a rule-based system. With sufficient determination all knowledge can be represented in rules as is regularly proven by implementors using commercial shells supporting only a rule-based formalism. Nevertheless, the availablity of frames, object-oriented and cooperative reasoning takes much of the drudgery out of system implementation. Where very complex reasoning must be supported, as in some high-level financial applications, the use of rules alone is inadequate and success depends on the use of alternative representations and mechanisms.

TRACKER replicated the reasoning of a methodical and well ordered engineering technician. In subsequent work it has been my privilege to examine the reasoning from financial and other professionals not coming from areas affected by the 'scientific paradigm'. In such areas, where there is sometimes little underlying rationale for what is done, the consequent representations and reasoning are rather more obscure. In such cases the prime objective is to replicate the expert's judgement even though its origin is not easily evident to the layman's eye.

USER INTERFACE

Considering that TRACKER was implemented without colour under CP/M, its user interface was a startling example of ingenuity. A single user model, that of an electronics technician experienced in the vocabulary and procedures of benchtop diagnosis (i.e. how to use test instruments and probe a circuit board) was implemented. The auxiliary help screens were based on this minimal competence model and did not support advice and explanations below its level. Thus the instruction to test an integrated circuit by substitution would assume that the technician was aware of all the associated heat damage problems and TRACKER did not offer detailed precautions on the use of heat sinks and desoldering tools etc.

All user interface interaction was via menus except for very limited natural language supporting replies of 'yes', 'no', 'twelve volts', etc. A block diagram graphical representation of major sub-assemblies of the power unit (e.g. transformers, PCBs, connector strips, etc) was laboriously constructed and proved of considerable use to technicians when identifying test and disconnection points etc. We seriously considered the use of interactive video and later purchased a videodisk unit and successfully interfaced it to TRACKER. Nevertheless, our experiment did not proceed due to the prohibitive cost of videodisk production.

Update

Apart from specific case details, user interaction is still largely via menus or cursor selection. Graphical selection is used where the delivery environment can support it and proves particularly useful to those experts who think in graphical terms.

Insofar as help screens and tracing facilities are involved, we now make extensive use of screen designs involving scrolling explanatory footnotes (with no need to push the F1 key) and graphical route maps which regularly show the user how he or she has progressed to their current state of dialogue and solution. These are particularly useful where it is required to hold and encourage the attention of the user during a long dialogue.

In the main I now assume that users are relatively unadventurous and that it is necessary to provide subsidiary material within 'glancing distance' without the need to consult auxiliary screens. The exception to this is the use of graphical interfaces where even the laziest user will soon learn to click on an icon representing the current focus of his or her interest.

ORGANIZATIONAL ISSUES

TRACKER would not have been produced if we had stuck to the rules. It was a full-scale research project originated by two organizationally unrelated line managers with no responsibility for research. The project was initially based solely on personal conviction and motivation. Nevertheless, as the initial work continued and became more obvious, it depended increasingly on the turning of blind eyes by our colleagues and the subtle misappropriation of budgets and time.

Following the success of the first TRACKER system we were legitimized and then most certainly had the approval, and a considerable degree of protection, from senior British Telecom management. However, subsequent TRACKER projects, using the shell generalised from the first project, were still conducted on a relatively flexible 'open-ended' basis without arduous budgetary control. Timescales were self-imposed and there remained an element of 'a solution looking for a problem' in our work. In other words, we were not answering an established demand for diagnostic support systems but were repeatedly seeking suitable cases where TRACKER could show its paces.

TRACKER is now a system of established use and utility to British Telecom. Developments are subject to rigorous budgetary control and the systems produced must meet real operational needs.

All the TRACKER systems were encoded using a Prolog-based shell. They were 'proper' expert systems according to all the accepted definitions. However, that first system, covering the power unit diagnosis, was based on diagnostic knowledge which was at the 'plateau' level and was unlikely to change. Our primary expert was well experienced with the particular power unit and was able to provide us with a more-or-less complete diagnostic breakdown.

For these reasons there is little doubt that the TRACKER algorithm could have been conventionally coded and the system would undoubtedly have run more efficiently if we had taken this course. Nevertheless, subsequent TRACKER implementations were based on knowledge which was incomplete and where the resulting systems would require regular incrementing. For these later systems the expert systems approach was entirely appropriate.

Similarly, all the work that I have been involved in since that first TRACKER system has been based on knowledge that was incomplete or subject to change. I have not come across any further instances of knowledge so well established that it could be considered as 'compiled' and so appropriate for hard-coding in a conventional language.

Update

In my current work cost–benefit analysis is an essential precursor to any expert systems project and the projects themselves are tightly managed using well established conventional project management tools.

The establishment of a Steering Group, particularly for a novel implementation, is very much recommended. If new expert systems software is to be used, or if a current shell is to be stretched to the limit, then the software provider should join the Steering Group and be responsible for any shell enhancements that may be necessary. In the case of TRACKER we were both shell providers and expert system implementors. Where these duties are made separate, as is now usually the case, there must be a proper apportionment of responsibility between those responsible for shell and knowledge base.

A 'champion' remains useful for an expert systems project but it is very necessary, especially for a long-duration implementation, to ensure that he is not the sole system patron. People move on and there have been several examples of projects (not my own) where a system has become stillborn with the loss of its lone senior sponsor.

Effective project management is necessary to ensure that commercial deliverables are realized on time and within budget. We were finding our way with TRACKER but, with a wealth of existing expert systems, there is no excuse not to manage expert systems projects with the same degree of precision as any conventional system implementation. Nevertheless, if one considers the slack in most conventional projects, it will be seen that the expert system practitioner can still rely on a small margin of sponsor's tolerance.

RETROSPECTIVE EVALUATION OF THE TRACKER PROJECT

TRACKER satisfied its main objectives of allowing George Pollard and I to prove ourselves and to persuade British Telecom to allow us to form the Knowledge Based Systems Unit. Further, the TRACKER system has proved to be of real practical use to British Telecom and, following the redesign and reimplementation exercise, now supports a wider range of tasks.

TRACKER was an appropriate product of its time, the project was a success and, even with hindsight, there is little that I would change about the way in which we undertook our tasks. The particular experience which we both gained was invaluable and, as has been already explained, has had profound implications for our subsequent work.

CONCLUSIONS

This account has centred upon a piece of work conducted some years ago at the commencement of the author's expert systems career. It should not be taken as an example of expert systems good practice although it is hoped that some of the contrasts with the author's subsequent and current work will be helpful in this respect.

TRACKER was fun and offered me the privilege of working with one of the most able of collaborators. Those aiming to start on their first expert systems projects are counselled to enjoy themselves even if this means that they must reserve proper authorization and budgetary justification for their second and subsequent projects!

RETROSPECTIVE EVALUATION OF THE TRACKER PROJECT

5

Expert Systems in Clarifying Employment Law

Mike Keen

ABSTRACT

The UK law relating to the dismissal of employees is complex and frequently misunderstood. In a collaborative venture, Expertech have worked with the city firm of accountants Robson Rhodes to develop a personal computer based expert system to clarify employment law for managers in small and medium sized companies. The system was the first substantial expert system application to be developed on a personal computer using a commercially available expert system 'shell'.

The author has been working on the development of expert systems since 1982, first at ICL and subsequently with Expertech which he joined as a founder member in 1984. At Expertech, he has been responsible for developing major expert system applications in a wide variety of areas, including both legal and financial systems. As a principal consultant, he is regularly involved in all aspects of the design and development of expert systems.

INTRODUCTION

The law regulating employment, and in particular that area dealing with the dismissal of employees, is complex and frequently misunderstood by many employers. In a collaborative undertaking, the expert system company Expertech worked with the city firm of accountants Robson Rhodes to develop an expert system to clarify employment law for managers in small and medium sized companies.

The expert system, 'Employment Law: Clarifying Dismissal', was developed as a joint effort by Robson Rhodes, who provided the domain expert in Employment Law—Steve McBride, and Expertech who supplied the knowledge engineer—the author. The system, which runs on IBM personal computers and IBM compatible machines, is marketed by the two organizations and is available from Expertech.

The original development of the system was carried out over a five month period, between December 1985 and April 1986, using Expertech's expert system shell 'Xi'. The approach adopted for developing the system was essentially one of incremental building, following on from the production of an initial prototype system for demonstration to management and potential users. During this building process, the expert from Robson Rhodes was very actively involved, both in drafting many of the rules himself and in testing the system extensively. The resulting system was one of the first substantial expert systems to be developed and run on personal computers, and certainly was the first such system to be developed using a commercially available expert system 'shell'.

Since its first release, the system has undergone quite major revision and updating. This has resulted partly from the introduction of a second expert from Robson Rhodes—Mandy Davis—onto the project, and partly due to changes in employment law itself. At the same time, various suggestions from users have been incorporated in the updated system. During this process of revision, the system has been reworked to take advantage of additional facilities that have been provided by subsequent releases of Expertech's 'Xi Plus' shell—the successor to the original 'Xi'.

OBJECTIVES

The law relating to dismissal

In the UK, there is a considerable body of legislation that regulates all aspects of employment. Much of this legislation is poorly understood, or not understood at all, by many employers.

One of the most difficult and complex areas of employment law is that relating to the dismissal of employees. Not only does it consist of statutory law, primarily from the Employment Protection (Consolidation) Act 1978, but also the results of many judgments made by Industrial Tribunals. Common law, as it relates to contracts of employment, complicates dismissal decisions still further.

Unfortunately, few employers are properly briefed on employment law and, other than in the larger organizations, rarely have trained professionals to whom they can turn in time of crisis.

The traditional sources of knowledge about employment law, the various textbooks on the subject, are far from easy reading for the non-specialist. In general, these books are structured so as to provide a statement of the law. This may be fine for the personnel professional who is reasonably familiar with the subject, but runs counter to the needs of an employer who is faced with the urgent need to make a decision on some employment matter, for example what disciplinary action to take following a fight on the factory floor. Another obvious direction to turn to for legal advice is solicitors, but there are few that specialize in cases of employment law.

So, when faced with the possibility of having to dismiss an employee, for whatever reason, many employers are ill-prepared to deal with the situation. This ignorance of the relevant law frequently leads them to avoid altogether making dismissal decisions for fear of falling foul of the law. At the heart of the matter is the worry that a dismissal may lead to a successful claim of 'unfair dismissal'.

Under UK law, most employees have the right not to be dismissed 'unfairly'. This does not mean that an employer cannot dismiss whomever he or she wants, but simply that if an employee has been dismissed 'unfairly', then that person has the right to be reinstated, re-engaged or compensated. What constitutes an 'unfair dismissal' is the subject of much of the law relating to dismissal.

If a dismissed employee makes a claim for unfair dismissal, the case may be heard by an Industrial Tribunal. Considerable amounts of management time can be consumed in preparing for the hearing. On top of this, there is the possibility of having to pay compensation to the dismissed employee if the dismissal is found to be 'unfair'.

The alternative to dismissal—retaining an employee who is not performing satisfactorily, or who is guilty of misconduct—may be equally disastrous, having an adverse effect on the performance of the business, or at least having a detrimental effect on other employees.

However, not all employers are so hesitant about dismissing an employee. A profound lack of understanding of an employer's legal responsibilities leads many of them into conflict with the law as a result of dismissing an employee unfairly. Even if there is a justifiable reason for dismissing someone, a failure to follow what is regarded as a fair disciplinary procedure, for instance by failing to allow the employee to explain his or her side of the case, is sufficient to result in a successful claim for unfair dismissal. From an employee's point of view, being dismissed unfairly is liable to result in a great deal of stress and unhappiness.

Thus, all employers have a need to be sure of their legal position when handling employee situations that might result in a dismissal. By following good practice procedures when dismissing an employee, employers can often avoid claims of unfair dismissal, or at least be in a better position to defend their actions should such a claim be made.

Stated objectives

Right from the beginning of the project, there was one clear basic aim behind the development of the 'Clarifying Dismissal' system. This was to provide a readily accessible source of advice for those who become involved in making decisions regarding the dismissal of an employee, but who are not specialists in the field and who have not received any special training in employment law. This concept was maintained right through development to the completion of the project.

It was recognized that there would be a wide variety of potential users for this system, including:

* Those running small businesses without personnel specialists, for whom the system would provide a practical alternative to reference books, to be consulted when faced with a possible decision to dismiss someone, or when redundancies are being considered.

* Line managers in large organizations with in-house personnel professionals, where the system could be used as a first step advisor to help them consider the relevant factors before consulting in-house.

Although the system was to be aimed primarily at employers, it was felt that employees' organizations, such as trade unions, and even individual employees would find the system useful and interesting to use, providing invaluable insight into legal rights in this area.

This diverse range of potential users meant that the system would have to provide both management and others with a basic understanding about the law, and to offer guidance and assistance in making decisions concerning individual employees and on overall management policies and procedures.

From these informal aims, a set of objectives was evolved for the system during the first few days of the project:

* to assist managers in understanding the fundamentals of the law as it applies to the dismissal of employees;

* to act as an advisor, to be consulted in respect of particular cases of potential dismissal; and

* to act as a training tool for all levels of management involved in decisions about staff discipline or in recommending that employees should be dismissed.

It was recognized that the system would not act as a substitute for professional advice, which can take into account the peculiarities particularly of the more complex cases. To this end, it was intended that the system would concentrate on straightforward cases of employment law, recognizing the trickier areas of the law and advising the user to seek professional advice in such cases.

Equally, the system was not intended to serve as a substitute for management judgement. In no way would it attempt to make decisions on behalf of management or to tell them what decisions to make. The 'Clarifying Dismissal' system was to advise and to inform the user of the system, to advise him or her of the likely consequences of a particular course of action, and possible pitfalls to avoid. At the same time, it was hoped that the system would be able to explain the legal principles involved, and impart some of this knowledge to the user.

Unstated objectives

There were further, unstated objectives of both partners in the project. For Robson Rhodes, the system would provide a vehicle for publicizing their Human Resources consultancy services, which include providing specialist advice on all aspects of employment law.

Equally, from Expertech's point of view, the system would demonstrate the capabilities of personal computer based expert systems. It should be remembered that, at the time that this system was being developed, there was almost universal scepticism regarding the use of personal computer based shells for the development of worthwhile expert systems.

Specification of requirements

An initial specification for the system was produced jointly by the senior management of the two partners in the development—Robson Rhodes and Expertech. However, this amounted to little more than a couple of paragraphs outlining what was perceived as the requirement for the system. At this point, there was no specific guidance given on the precise areas of dismissal law that were to be covered by the system or on the form of treatment that was to be afforded to the material.

However, it was specified that the first stage of development was to confirm the overall feasibility of the system and to clarify the system requirement by developing an initial demonstration of the application. Two weeks were allowed for this task, due to the desirability of making a firm decision on whether to proceed before Christmas 1985. Although this timescale seemed tight, the close proximity of the first deadline forced those assigned to the project to get on with the job without delay.

During those first two weeks of work, there was a great deal of learning, the knowledge engineer learning about employment law, and the expert learning about expert systems. By the end of those first two weeks, both parties were in a much better position to define the requirements for the final system.

The prototype system that was produced during those first two weeks encompassed approximately 20% of the anticipated domain knowledge. Demonstrating it to senior management helped them see much more clearly how expert systems could be applied to this type of problem and so to clarify what was required of the eventual system. At the same time, the opportunity was taken to demonstrate the system to a professional personnel adviser to gain an independent reaction to the system.

So, after two weeks development of an initial demonstration prototype, the knowledge engineer and expert were in agreement and able to specify quite clearly the functionality that was required of the final system. That this was not formally written out in detail might seem surprising, but by this stage sufficient time had been spent discussing the requirements that each was satisfied that the other knew what was required. However, the structure of the eventual system was mapped out as a series of diagrams, allocating aspects of the system to individual knowledge bases. These diagrams became the basis for all future work.

From this point on, the view of what was required from the eventual system did not alter fundamentally as the project progressed.

Initial evaluation criteria

It was agreed that the criteria by which the performance of the system would be judged would be that the system must:

— be perceived by users as being relevant to the problems that they have to deal with;

— be usable by those with no prior knowledge of either expert systems or employment law;

— be able to advise on all the commonly occurring and straightforward dismissal situations; and

— not mislead its users.

As a corollary to the above, it was recognized that certain cases, for instance those involving possible allegations of racial or sexual discrimination, can be particularly difficult to handle, and for such cases the user would be advised to seek further professional advice.

Hardware and software

For the 'Clarifying Dismissal' system to be of practical use, it had to be deliverable on hardware and software that was widely available. That meant that the preferred delivery vehicle had to be the IBM Personal Computer and compatible machines. However, at the time the system was being proposed, late in 1985, such machines offered very much less performance than the '286' and '386' personal computers of 1989.

Equally, the choice of development software, Expertech's first shell 'Xi', was very much on the basis that it was the only shell available, either on personal computers or on larger machines, that held out any prospect of being suitable for a system of the size and complexity of the application being planned.

However on both counts, choice of hardware and software, the system was very much a leap into the unknown, there being no experience with comparable systems being built and run on personal computers, or on any other hardware for that matter.

In fact, two delivery versions of the final system were eventually made available:

(i) a set of knowledge bases ready to run using the standard 'Xi' shell; and

(ii) a fully packaged version of the system based around a cut down run-time only version of 'Xi'.

Subsequently, the system was converted to run under 'Xi Plus' when this was released, and the fully packaged version of the system was based around 'Xi User', the run-time only version of 'Xi Plus'. Both with 'Xi' and later with 'Xi Plus', no additional knowledge engineering was required to produce the fully packaged version, the knowledge bases etc. being fully portable between the development and run-time only environments.

Since the application was intended to be completely free-standing, the question of interfacing with other software did not really arise. Although it would have been feasible to interface, for instance, to a personnel database, it was felt that there would be so little relevant information already held on such databases, that it would not be worthwhile.

DEVELOPING THE SYSTEM

An exploratory approach

The approach taken when developing an application such as the 'Clarifying Dismissal' expert system is quite unlike that used in producing conventional software systems. Conventional software is the result of a series of decisions by the designer. In developing a system such as this, one is not attempting to create or design something new. The essence of the system, the experience in interpreting and applying employment law, already exists in the mind of the expert. The development process becomes one of exploring his know-how and recording the experiences encountered. A process that is made easier by the very act of writing down the expert's knowledge.

Similarly, the way in which the expert's knowledge is brought together and structured is heavily influenced by the way the expert views his domain of expertise and how he tackles individual problems, and not by some *a priori* logical way of doing it.

This exploration of the complex and initially unstructured knowledge of the expert leads to a style of building that involves 'incremental development'. Rather than attempting to produce a comprehensive and detailed specification at the outset, an initial prototype of part of the system is first produced based on a simple statement of objectives. This is then extended and refined over repeated iterations, with the content and hence capabilities of the system growing progressively.

The shell chosen for this development—'Xi', and later 'Xi Plus'—had been designed to support this approach to development. Rules are input directly into the system and are immediately available to be run and tested, there being no separate compilation stage. This provides a sense of immediacy and responsiveness to the building process. It also means that the developer can enter an incomplete set of rules into the system, in the full knowledge that later correction will not cause problems. Equally, the input of elements of the know-how can be deferred until such a time as the know-how is better understood.

From start to finish, the process of developing the 'Clarifying Dismissal' system consisted of the following stages:

Idea
   ⇒Prototype
      ⇒Demonstration
         ⇒Incremental development
           of full system
               ⇒Validation &
                User Trials
  ⇐Feasibility⇒

Feasibility demonstration

During the development of the system, prototypes were used for two principal purposes:

— to confirm the feasibility of the system; and

— as an aid to eliciting the expert's know-how.

They were also used to help refine the user interface. By showing prototypes of the system to potential users at an early stage in development, valuable feedback was obtained regarding the way that the system was presenting itself to users.

Confirming feasibility

Following a joint decision by Robson Rhodes and Expertech to explore the possibility of building an expert system to advise on employment law, work began early in December 1985. The first two weeks of project development were spent building up a prototype of the proposed system that could be demonstrated to management.

From the start it was agreed that the expert would play a very active role in the whole process. Although the initial discussions with the expert were very much 'paper based', these rapidly gave way first to live input of the rules in the presence of the expert, and then to the expert producing a first draft of the rules himself. A style of working quickly evolved whereby the expert produced a set of draft rules covering a particular aspect of the problem, and then the knowledge engineer refined these to form part of a working knowledge base.

For the first two or three days, progress was faltering as each person learnt about the other's expertise—the knowledge engineer about employment law and the expert about expert systems. Thereafter progress was rapid. After just 7 days effort by each of the parties, and several iterations, a three knowledge base feasibility demonstration was complete. This comprised:

* A simple introductory knowledge base.
* A knowledge base on Unfair Dismissal, dealing with the issues of eligibility to claim unfair dismissal and fairness of the dismissal itself.
* A knowledge base to assess the likely remedies and compensation resulting from a successful claim for unfair dismissal.

The whole system amounted to some 200 rules.

This first demonstration system was shown to management just before Christmas, and was more than sufficient to convince them that:

— the nature of the task was suitable for implementing as an expert system;
— the necessary expertise was available and that the expert was sufficiently articulate;
— the expert's knowledge could be represented using the symbolic rule based approach of 'Xi';
— the size and complexity of the task was within the capabilities of 'Xi' running on a personal computer;
— the effort that would be required to complete the system seemed to be acceptable; and
— the resulting system would be relevant to the needs of the target users.

As well as being used to demonstrate the feasibility of the overall system, the prototype was used to gain detailed feedback from management and potential users about the type of system that was being planned. This helped improve the focus of the system.

At the time of the demonstration, it was estimated that the initial prototype contained a quarter of all the relevant knowledge about the law on dismissal. The correct proportion subsequently turned out to be about a fifth—i.e. 20%.

From the preceding description, one might gain the impression that building the 'Clarifying Dismissal' system was no more than the development of a series of prototypes. In fact, the development was really incremental in nature, the initial rule set providing the first increment and then development proceeding by building on and extending from this in a series of stages. Even the demonstration prototype was really the product of a number of incremental stages, rather than a one-off prototype.

Knowledge elicitation

All the knowledge elicitation was carried out at Expertech's offices at Slough, which provided a convenient refuge for the expert away from the constant interruptions of his normal working environment.

At the very first meeting with the expert, the knowledge engineer took time to explain the concepts of expert systems. This started with a demonstration of several existing systems in various application areas, and then the actual process of rule input was demonstrated. (This was helped by the fact that the expert had some limited computer experience, having done some programming in his university days.) Then the discussion moved to employment law.

Although the initial discussions with the expert involved much drawing of diagrams on paper and the hand drafting of rules, this rapidly gave way to the knowledge engineer inputting rules in front of the expert—virtually with the expert dictating them.

The flexibility for building offered by the 'Xi' shell meant that initially the expert and knowledge engineer were able to select a particular area of interest—such as establishing eligibility to claim unfair dismissal—and very quickly build up a basic set of rules to cover the chosen topic. This initial rule set was far from complete even in the context of very limited coverage of the chosen topic. For instance, it asked questions for the sake of convenience rather than because these were the right questions to ask of the user. Subsequent iterations then added further levels of rules until the appropriate questions could be asked.

The expert came to understand what was required very quickly, and was soon producing a first draft of the rules himself—but using a word processor rather than 'Xi' itself. A style of working quickly evolved whereby the expert produced a set of draft rules covering a particular aspect of the problem. He then handed these draft rules over to the knowledge engineer who refined and rephrased them as necessary to form a working prototype. This prototype was then shown to the expert and, invariably, this led to him identifying gaps and misunderstandings which needed to be resolved. He then detailed the changes that needed to be made and the prototype was amended. The whole process was repeated until a set of rules had been produced that satisfied both the expert and the knowledge engineer.

Soon, the expert was able to explore a knowledge base by himself, using the shell's explanation facilities to view the rules being used. Sometimes this process triggered the expert into volunteering some additional information which exposed a whole new dimension to the problem in hand that had previously been overlooked.

As the main system development involved just one expert, there was no question of conflict between experts. Later, during system validation when other experts were reviewing the system, there were disagreements, but these were always resolved by discussion between the experts. Later still, when a second expert was introduced on to the project, there were more fundamental disagreements, but these were resolved by the two experts talking the issues through with the knowledge engineer to reach a common agreed point of view. As part of this process of resolving differences, actually amending the existing system was found to be a useful way of showing one expert the ideas being put forward by the other.

Judging by the experts' reaction to the whole elicitation process, one can safely say that they both enjoyed it, and were stimulated by it.

Building the system

Once the feasibility of the proposed system had been demonstrated successfully, the main system development was able to proceed. Again, rather than attempt to produce a comprehensive system specification of what was required, the expert and knowledge engineer worked from their refined understanding of the objectives of the system.

Working together, an overall structure was first devised for the final system—identifying the individual knowledge bases, their respective roles, and how they would link together. This process was based on the use of simple 'block' diagrams. Each of the knowledge bases was then examined and the individual tasks within each knowledge base were identified and mapped out, again using a diagrammatic approach.

Each knowledge base was then built up in turn. The knowledge base maps were used to select individual tasks which were then explored in detail with the aim of completing each of these, without leaving any holes.

$$\text{Map-out} \Rightarrow \text{Build} \Rightarrow \quad \text{Test \&} \quad \Rightarrow \text{Completed}$$
$$\text{tasks} \qquad \text{task} \quad \Rightarrow \text{review} \qquad \text{task}$$
$$\qquad \qquad \qquad \text{Enhance} \Leftarrow$$
$$\qquad \qquad \qquad \text{\& refine}$$

As each task was considered, a set of rules was produced and added to the relevant knowledge base, expanding the content and hence capabilities of that knowledge base. Along with the rules, the corresponding user questions had also to be defined. A further time-consuming activity was the drafting of the text used by the system to explain points of employment law and for giving advice.

Each set of additions was tested by the knowledge engineer as soon as they were added to the system to make sure that they were working as intended, and that there were no obvious presentation problems—such as spelling mistakes or poor layout of text. The expert also reviewed the area of the system currently being developed on a regular basis—often daily. Generally, this reviewing involved the expert running the system and using the system's explanation facilities to look at the rules being used.

Due to the exploratory nature of this form of incremental development, the organization of the individual knowledge bases was subject to constant revision and tended to become physically 'untidy'. However, this danger was recognized, and as a better understanding was gained of the expert's knowledge in any particular case, the knowledge base was reorganized to keep it tidy. This process was generally overlapped with ongoing incremental development to produce what was hopefully a complete and well organized knowledge base at the end.

As work progressed, the system structure was kept under review and a number of changes made:

— it was found to be more convenient to divide the handling of unfair dismissal into three knowledge bases, rather than the two as originally planned; and

— it was decided that a separate knowledge base covering 'pregnancy and confinement' was unnecessary.

The actual process of building the main knowledge bases proceeded very quickly. By the end of February, the 10 main knowledge bases were all built, running, and linked together. By this point, the total system had grown to some 900 rules.

Now, the entire system was ready for the expert to review it in detail—particularly with respect to the correctness and completeness of the advice that it gave. Once each knowledge base had been reviewed, the necessary amendments were made by the knowledge engineer. This review and testing process resulted in quite major surgery to several of the knowledge bases, but this was accomplished without drama.

At the same time that the expert was reviewing the nearly completed system, the knowledge engineer was carrying out extensive mechanical testing of each knowledge base, looking for holes in the knowledge. At the same time, the quality of finish of the system was scrutinized closely—it being very time-consuming to ensure that a system of this size is virtually free of typing errors, spelling mistakes and other trivial errors. No sooner does it seem that the system is free of errors than somebody finds one more.

This reviewing process was completed by the beginning of April, and the complete system was then released to a number of target users for a month's 'beta testing'.

Involvement of the users

The developers' first real involvement with potential users of the system was after the first two weeks when the demonstration version of the system was shown to management and others. Thereafter, as the system was being developed it was regularly shown to members of staff in both organizations to obtain feedback.

Right at the beginning of development, when the system was first shown to users, they were asked to comment on the overall aims and objectives of the system, and on the approach being taken, the style of the consultation, and so on. Then, as development progressed, additional and more detailed comment was sought on the form that the consultation was taking—the wording and sequence of the questions being asked, and on the reporting of conclusions.

A further issue on which comment was sought was the degree of explanation built into the system, and the balance between the explanations contained in the text of questions and any supplementary explanation available on request.

At all stages, those who tried out the system were quick to point out any problems with the knowledge engineering, from situations where the system failed to reach a conclusion, right down to spelling mistakes in the text of questions.

Another area where user input was invaluable was in building the tutorial knowledge base that gives a general overview of the law on dismissal. Here, it was vital to achieve the right balance between the explanations being provided and the games used to test the users' understanding. Above all else, this knowledge base had to be fun to run through and avoid being boring.

Much later, towards the end of development, a number of possible users of the system were identified as 'beta test' users of the system. At this stage, with the system nearing completion, the input being sought was very much concerned with their view of the system's final fitness for purpose.

Later updating and enhancement

Following the initial release of the system, a few very minor errors were identified by customers running the system. As luck would have it, the builders also found a few more spelling errors after release.

A few months later, towards the end of 1986, Robson Rhodes recruited a personnel consultant with very extensive industrial experience of employment law—Mandy Davis—and she was asked to review the system. This review started by simply running test cases through the system, but rapidly developed into a thorough examination of the rules and all the associated text. At this point, the effort that had been put into producing readable rules helped enormously, and the new recruit was very quickly able to make sense of—and comment on—the inner workings of the knowledge bases.

The comments that resulted from this review provided the basis for a possible set of enhancements to the system.

By this time, Expertech had released its new shell 'Xi Plus' and the original system had been quickly converted, though not released, to run on this new product. With the prospect of various forthcoming changes to the law on employment, including changes resulting from a recent European Court ruling on retirement ages, a joint decision was taken to update the system.

Working largely with, and taking into account the comments and suggestions of the second expert, a totally revised system was produced over the next three months. With a target of having the revised system available in time for the changes in the law, approximately 25 days effort was put in by the expert and knowledge engineer during this period.

The effects of the changes in the law were really quite minor and were accommodated with about a day's effort. Much more significant were some of the new expert's suggestions, which resulted in significant reorganization of parts of the system, with the interfaces between certain knowledge bases being subtly redefined. At the same time as all this was going on, the original simplistic conversion from 'Xi' to 'Xi Plus' was reworked to take advantage of new facilities—in particular 'demons'— that had been introduced with 'Xi Plus'.

Following all this change, the complete system had to be retested to make sure that it still worked correctly, and this was probably the most time consuming aspect of the whole process. The revised system was then released, and updates provided for those who had purchased the original version of the system.

More recently, during 1988, the system has again undergone major revision. This time the underlying knowledge was unchanged, but the entire user interface has been reworked to take into account the screen building facility known as 'forms' that had been introduced with 'Xi Plus'. This task was given to a second knowledge engineer who had not previously worked with the system. The work was supervised by the author, and the only significant problem encountered was due to the colour blindness of the second knowledge engineer!

This revised version of the system is scheduled to be released shortly, to run under Release 3 of 'Xi Plus'.

Resources, effort and timescales

The overall plan for developing the 'Clarifying Dismissal' system was to use an experienced knowledge engineer (the author) full time, with the expert being available for an average of three days per week, and this balance of effort was followed throughout the project. The unusually high degree of involvement by the expert reflected the initial management decision that the expert should play a very active role in the development of the system. Certainly, it contributed to the relatively short development timescales.

The breakdown of the work during the period from December 1985 to April 1986 is as follows:

* The first feasibility stage of the development took 14 man days—7 by each of the expert and the knowledge engineer. This produced three knowledge bases, totalling some 200 rules.

* The main building phase took 35 man days—14 by the expert and 21 by the knowledge engineer—and resulted in 10 knowledge bases and more than 900 rules.

* The final checking and 'polishing' to beta test level took a total of 21 man days—7 by the expert and 14 by the knowledge engineer—and took the system to over 1000 rules.

Up to the time of beta testing, when the system really was virtually complete, the system consisted of:

10 linked knowledge bases, 1030 rules, 263 questions, and 150 kb of explanatory text.

During the subsequent revisions to the system, the effort involved was not monitored so closely, and it would be misleading to quote any detailed figures for this work. However, one slightly surprising figure did emerge from the conversion of the system from 'Xi' to 'Xi Plus'. By taking advantage of the enhanced facilities of the new system, the overall size of the system actually fell to approximately 950 rules—despite the increased functionality resulting from the enhancements to the system.

THE 'CLARIFYING DISMISSAL' SYSTEM

System structure

By the time that the demonstration had been developed, a clear picture had emerged of the overall structure required of the system. At the top-most level, the system quite naturally divided into three main topic areas:

— the provision of an overview of dismissal law in the form of a tutorial for those unfamiliar with employment law;

— the handling of all aspects of unfair dismissal; and

— dealing with all the issues relating to dismissal of redundant employees.

In turn, handling cases of unfair dismissal was identified as being intrinsically a three-stage process:

(i) determining whether an employee is entitled to claim unfair dismissal;

(ii) establishing whether the dismissal itself was unfair, for instance because there was no fair reason, or because the dismissal procedure had been unfair; and

(iii) calculating the likely compensation to be awarded by an industrial tribunal in a case of unfair dismissal.

This breakdown formed the basis for partitioning the unfair dismissal part of the system into individual knowledge bases with all straightforward cases of unfair dismissal being handled by three knowledge bases according to the three stages listed above. In fact, two additional knowledge bases were included to deal with the complex and specialized situations of dismissal on the grounds of 'lack of capability' and 'lack of qualifications', and of 'misconduct'—though these were both closely integrated with the three main unfair dismissal knowledge bases.

In a very similar way, the handling of redundancy matters also partitioned itself quite naturally into three separate knowledge bases.

Control within each knowledge base was largely organized around the backward chaining of 'Xi', supplemented by limited use of the forward chaining available in the product. Later, with the availability of 'Xi Plus', forward chaining demons became available and these were used extensively to improve the system's responsiveness—for instance to handle requests for an additional explanation or even to alter the course of the whole consultation.

System description

The 'Clarifying Dismissal' system does not attempt to encode the law directly. Instead, it uses expert knowledge about interpreting the law and emulates the advice that such an expert would give to others.

The first knowledge base introduces the system for the new user, explaining how to use its facilities. It also identifies and loads the next knowledge base that the user requests. A second knowledge base—'Dismissal Overview'—provides an introductory tutorial on the principles of dismissal and provides an introduction to the other knowledge bases in the system.

Three knowledge bases deal with cases of unfair dismissal, covering:

* The eligibility of an employee to claim for unfair dismissal.

* Whether the real reason for dismissing an employee is likely to be

considered fair or unfair, and whether the dismissal procedure used appears to be a fair one.

* The likely costs to the employer if a claim for unfair dismissal is successful.

Two further knowledge bases deal with major reasons for dismissal: misconduct and poor performance.

* The 'Misconduct' knowledge base explores whether dismissal on the basis of misconduct is fair, before going on to consider the fairness of the dismissal procedure used by the employer.

* The 'Capability' knowledge base explores whether dismissal on the basis of lack of capability or lack of qualifications—including such problems as lack of competence, absence due to illness, and inability to meet performance targets—is likely to be considered fair. It also goes on to examine the fairness of the procedure used to dismiss the employee.

Dismissal on the grounds of 'Redundancy' is dealt with by a further three knowledge bases which:

* Help to decide whether the dismissal of a particular employee falls into the definition of redundancy.

* Review the statutory procedures for redundancy situations, and provide an overview of the recommended policies which employers should adopt in relation to redundancy.

* Compute the statutory minimum redundancy payment.

At the end of each stage in the consultation, the user is asked to choose what he wants to do next, and the appropriate next knowledge base is loaded automatically.

Representation and reasoning

Part of the decision to develop the system using 'Xi' was a belief that its powerful symbolic processing capabilities, within a straightforward production rule structure would prove ideally suited to the needs of the 'Clarifying Dismissal' system, and so it proved.

The following few rules, dealing with unfair dismissal, are sufficient to demonstrate the type and style of the knowledge used in the system. The first rule is at a high level and is one of several that are used to decide whether the dismissal of an employee is likely to be considered fair:

> if the employee is eligible to claim unfair dismissal
> and reason for dismissal is likely to be considered fair
> and dismissal procedure is fair
> then dismissal of the employee is likely to be considered fair

This rule has three conditions that have to be satisfied before the conclusion of the rule can be drawn. Evaluation of each of these conditions is illustrated by the following three rules—though these are by no means the only rules that could be used to infer these particular conclusions:

> if work relationship is under a contract of employment
> and contract termination is by dismissal
> and employment category is not excluded from unfair dismissal
> and hours worked is sufficient to qualify
> and period of service is long enough to qualify
> and age on dismissal is less than the normal retiring age
> then the employee is eligible to claim unfair dismissal

> if principal reason for dismissal is gross misconduct
> and time of misconduct is within working hours
> then reason for dismissal is likely to be considered fair

> if principal reason for dismissal is other than redundancy
> and action of employer is fair and reasonable
> then dismissal procedure is fair

In turn, these three rules, and others like them, depend on a whole set of further conditions being proved. At this level, most of the conditions depend on the proving of other rules, although some of them—such as 'work relationship' and 'time of misconduct'—are directly asked of the user.

Typical of these lower level rules would be:

> if the number of employees is more than 20
> and length of continuous service is not less than 1 year
> then period of service is long enough to qualify

Each of the conditions of this rule are asked directly of the user by means of a question. For example:

> How many people are employed by the employer, and any associated employers?
> [] more than 20
> [] between 5 and 20
> [] 5 or less

Two particular points stand out from these sample rules:

1. The overall readability of these rules is so good that anyone with a basic understanding of the subject—i.e. unfair dismissal—would have no difficulty understanding the logic of a particular rule. This is not by accident.

2. There is no obvious sign that the wording of the rules has been abbreviated for any particular reason, and this is indeed the case.

When building the system, particular care was taken both to write the rules using the words of the expert, and to phrase the rules in such a way as to make the rules read like English language statements. This results in an obvious improvement to the standard 'why?' and 'how?' explanations which involve 'Xi'/'Xi Plus' displaying the rules of the knowledge base.

More important, however, is the impact that this careful phrasing of rules has on the ability of the expert (and other experts) to read through the rules as part of the validation process. By this means, the expert's involvement in testing and validation was extended beyond simple exercising of the system to include him actually reading through all the knowledge bases. Experience on this project, and other subsequent projects, has shown that this can be a very effective additional means of testing knowledge bases.

Another point that can be seen by looking at the example rules is the manner with which uncertainty is handled. The model used was entirely one of following the style of conclusion being drawn by the expert and this produced conclusions such as:

> 'reason for dismissal is likely to be considered fair'

No attempt was made to quantify the degree of likelihood since the expert did not attempt this himself. Thus, the approach closely mirrored the advice that an expert in this field would expect to provide.

User interface

The target users of the system were envisaged as being middle to senior level managers, many of whom would not be regular computer users. Equally, it could safely be assumed that many users would start off being largely ignorant of the subject matter of the system—the law on dismissal. In fact, it was felt that the system should be suitable for use by those with no prior knowledge—either of using computers or of the law on dismissal.

To meet the needs of these target users, the system interface needed to be easy to use and devoid of 'kimmicks'—both in computer terms and in terms of assumptions regarding prior knowledge of the law on dismissal. However, simply designing a system for those with no prior experience could so very easily produce a system that would be found to be laborious by those with experience, with the danger that they would 'switch off' very rapidly and be unwilling to use the system. It is also important to remember that users who start off with no prior knowledge might be expected to become familiar with using the system, and with aspects of the law on dismissal simply by using the system. Thus, while they may start off quite satisfied with an interface designed for beginners, they would rapidly outgrow this and find the system pedestrian.

The solution to this apparent conflict of requirements was to:

— include a basic tutorial at the very beginning of the system to teach the real beginner how to physically operate the system—answer questions, and so on;

— provide a separate and quite extensive tutorial on employment law, explaining the underlying terminology and concepts (as was described earlier, this was provided as a separate knowledge base);

— make periodic use of text explanations to tell the user what is going on—introducing each stage of the consultation, reporting conclusions that have been reached, and so on;

— use a predominantly menu form of questioning; and

— provide copious supplementary explanations, selectable by the user.

All explanations were based on the use of standard text files, which later 'Xi Plus' allowed to be managed using a simple library facility. (This was particularly important for this type of system with more than a hundred text files running to about 150 kb of text.) Extensive use was made of the 'Xi' facility to substitute inferred values in text being reported to the user. At one level, this allowed all text to be tailored to reflect the gender of the person being considered for dismissal, substituting 'she' for 'he', 'her' for 'him', etc. and so avoiding the horrible alternative of 'he/she' which so often appears in written material.

In a system of this type, there is no place for simple one line conclusions of the form:

'sack the blaggard'!!!

and substitution of inferred values also enabled comprehensive reporting of conclusions, without the need to produce separate reports for every conceivable combination of conclusions.

Although the system made extensive use of text for providing explanations and descriptions, by its very nature the application did not warrant the use of graphics or video displays, etc. though both are available with 'Xi Plus'.

The use of a menu style of questioning, although not considered particularly glamorous in some quarters, does offer a number of distinct advantages over natural language input. In particular:

— it reduces the typing required of users who are not experienced at using a keyboard to the absolute minimum and with a little care in ordering menus, so that the most frequently selected option appears at the head of the list, very few keystrokes are needed for a complete consultation;

— the menu options form part of the question text and help explain the question, leaving no uncertainty as to what is expected by way of an answer from the user.

Supplementary explanations were provided, again using preformated text, both to:

— explain concepts and ideas; and
— provide additional explanations on questions.

Some of this was provided in response to the use of the 'help' key— F1—but much more was made available via additional options on the question menus, of the form:

[] . . .
[] . . .
[] please explain terms

By putting the 'offer' of additional explanation as one of the question options, the system was able to use quite succinct question text that was suitable for the more experienced user. However, the beginner would not be left 'without any visible means of support' and would only need to select the very obvious explanation option to receive a much fuller statement of what was required.

Another aspect required of the user interface was to protect the user from the internal complexities of the system so that he or she would not need to know how to navigate around the system between knowledge bases, or how to rerun knowledge bases. All the necessary control, and it really was not very much, was built into the knowledge bases themselves, with the user being asked to make simple choices of direction at key points in the consultation.

Due to the target audience for this system, it was felt vital that the system achieved a high degree of polish—i.e. that it be presented to the highest possible standard, free of spelling, punctuation or other grammatical errors, with a high level of consistency throughout the system in terms of layout of questions and reports. To this end, a very considerable amount of time was spent in the latter stages of development in polishing the user interface to achieve this required level of presentation.

Much later, following the conversion of the system to run under 'Xi Plus', the introduction of the 'Xi Plus' 'forms' facility allowed a fundamental rebuilding of the user interface. Although still based on the principles described above, the additional facilities provided with 'forms' allowed many improvements to be made. Whereas with 'Xi', and early releases of 'Xi Plus', only a single question or text explanation could appear on the screen at one time, the use of 'Xi Plus' 'forms' allows much greater freedom. The user interface of the latest version of the 'Clarifying Dismissal' system has taken advantage of this, for example to:

— build up dynamic question sequences on the screen, so that the user is able to see the answers that he or she gave to earlier questions in the consultation sequence; and

— display the text of a conclusion alongside the sequence of questions that led to that conclusion being inferred.

As well as the obvious improvements in quality of presentation resulting from the use of 'Xi Plus' 'forms', the ability to display a complete question sequence and the following conclusion helps the user gain a better understanding of the underlying reasoning.

EVALUATION OF PERFORMANCE

Testing and validation

Throughout the building process, testing of the system was carried out continuously:

— incremental testing by the knowledge engineer to ensure that the developing system actually worked, and that it worked as he thought it should;

— regular reviewing of the system by the expert, with him running the system and examining both the rules and all the associated text— both in questions and conclusions, and that used to provide explanations.

Further and more exhaustive testing was carried out by the knowledge engineer on completion of each knowledge base to make sure that everything worked as intended, both at the level of individual knowledge bases and with sequences of knowledge bases linked together.

System validation really started with a further extensive review of the completed knowledge bases by the expert. This involved him running test cases through the system, using the knowledge bases in their correct sequences, to check that the final conclusions being reached were correct.

In fact, there was considerable overlap between the parts of the processes described above since the initial validation of one part of the system might identify problems requiring surgery by the knowledge engineer, who then modified the knowledge base(s) concerned, before the whole cycle was repeated.

Generally, testing and validation did not stop as soon as a problem was found, unless it was really fundamental, and changes were usually noted as they were identified and applied to knowledge bases in batches. Throughout this process, both the knowledge engineer and the expert were checking to ensure the system was achieving the required level of polish.

With the system fast approaching a state where both the knowledge engineer and expert were satisfied with its performance, the expert arranged for the system to be reviewed by a small number of other experts in the field of employment law. The peer group members were identified by the expert himself as people whom he recognized as being especially knowledgeable in the particular field. All but one member of this group was external to the developers—Robson Rhodes and Expertech—and so the members of the group had to be selected both on the basis of their undoubted experience and expertise in the field, and also on the likelihood of their actually completing the review and producing comments on the system. The group included both practising personnel professionals and a lecturer in employment law.

This peer group made use of their extensive live case experience when evaluating the system. This process produced a large number of comments—most of which related to points of detail, and in particular to points of emphasis within the explanatory texts. By the time that the final comments had been received, and appropriate modifications and additions had been made to the system, it was capable of handling all the test cases successfully.

A further aspect of validation that was carried out as the system was being developed was to assess the suitability of the system for its target audience. From time to time, beginners—particularly those who knew nothing about employment law—were sat down with the system and asked to try it out. From the comments received, it was concluded that the approach being adopted was the right one, but the feedback enabled a certain amount of fine tuning to be carried out.

Use in practice

Since the system was launched in the spring of 1986, it has been bought by a number of organizations. Initially, it seemed that many customers quite simply bought the application as a demonstration of what could be achieved using 'Xi' on a personal computer—and for this they seemed admirably satisfied by the system. However, among the customers there have been quite a number of sales to personnel departments and for use by line managers.

With a system of this type, where the system is to be used by a customer organization, it is difficult to obtain much feedback from users. However, those who have taken the trouble to comment back have expressed their satisfaction and generally confirmed that the system has met its original objectives.

There remains the suspicion that some organizations have used the system more in a training role, to make managers more aware of their legal responsibilities in matters relating to employment law, but there is no concrete evidence on which to base this.

LESSONS AND CONCLUSIONS

Expert systems on PCs

To appreciate some of the lessons from the development of the 'Clarifying Dismissal' system one has to recall the level of experience—both with the use of personal computers for expert systems and with the use of expert system shells—that existed at the time that the system was being developed. At that time, few if any serious expert systems had been developed on personal computers and certainly none using an 'off the shelf' expert system shell.

The development of the 'Clarifying Dismissal' system was a clear demonstration of the suitability of personal computers for substantial expert system tasks—at first release, the system comprised more than 1000 rules. It was apparent to anyone using the system that it contained a very substantial body of knowledge, and that this was expressed in a form that is very easy to use.

That the system was built using an 'off the shelf' expert system shell made the development all the more important. The fact that at no stage in the development process was any significant problem encountered either with the 'Xi' shell itself or in matching it to the needs of building a system to clarify employment law simply served to underline the potential of personal computer based shells.

The system also demonstrated for the first time the suitability of expert systems techniques for clarifying the law for the less experienced.

That much of the above is now taken for granted, and that most expert systems being delivered for operational use today have been developed to run on personal computers using shells, simply serves to emphasize the pioneering nature of the development of the original 'Clarifying Dismissal' system.

Lessons in knowledge engineering

The incremental approach taken to development was undoubtedly a major contributory factor in the success of the whole exercise. It enabled the expert to review the development of the system at every stage and so make sure that the knowledge engineer was correctly recording his know-how.

The especially close involvement of the expert throughout the process served to enhance the advantages of incremental development. At no time during development was the knowledge engineer left waiting because of lack of availability of the expert. Indeed, the opposite did occur with the knowledge engineer being inundated with draft rules from the expert and then keeping the expert waiting for a working prototype. The expert's close involvement was also of considerable advantage in the translation of the legal jargon into language understandable by a non-specialist.

From the very beginning, it was apparent that the intended system would be quite large—the initial estimate was that it would involve at least 800 rules. By structuring the system and dividing it up into separate knowledge bases, with no more than 150 rules in any one, problems associated with large individual knowledge bases—such as testing and amending—were largely avoided.

Taken overall, the development process was so successful—meeting objectives and deadlines in a highly innovative situation—that it would be hard to justify any significant change of approach, given the same circumstances all over again. Perhaps the one area where the original version of the system was lacking was in screen presentation—though this is now only apparent with very considerable hindsight, and following the availability of enhanced presentation facilities in expert system shells generally. This problem has now been remedied in the latest version of the system that uses 'Xi Plus' 'forms'.

BIBLIOGRAPHY

On Employment law

Janner's Consolidated Compendium of Employment Law, Business Books.

Tolly's Employment Handbook—3rd Edition, Tolly Publishing Co.

Payne, D. *Employment Law Manual plus Case Law Supplement*, Gower Press, London.

Anderman, S. D. *The Law of Unfair Dismissal*—2nd Edition, Butterworths, Guildford.

Selwyn, N. M. *Selwyn's Law of Employment*—5th Edition, Butterworths, Guildford.

On the 'Clarifying Dismissal' system

Keen and McBride (1986). *Expert Systems in Clarifying Employment Law*, Proceedings of KBS'86, Online Publications.

On the development of commercial expert systems in general.

Barrett and Beerel. *Expert Systems in Business*, Ellis Horwood.

6

Intelligent Data Interpretation

Rob Milne

ABSTRACT

This is the story of a failure and a success. Both projects involved the use of expert systems for interpreting data about the condition of a process or plant in manufacturing. In the first project, *monitoring a process control system*, a number of key lessons are learned, identifying why process monitoring is a particularly hard problem for expert systems today. In the second system, *determining the condition of rotating machinery based on its vibration*, expert systems are ideally suited for the task. A cost-effective and successful system was built very quickly. By exploring the differences between these two applications, we identify a number of critical aspects of successful expert systems.

INTRODUCTION

Our work at Intelligent Applications is focussed on the near-term application of expert systems technology to manufacturing-related problems. In particular, we focus on the task of data interpretation. Existing factory data acquisition systems merely collect data and provide a display of the raw information. The most elaborate systems provide data browsing capabilities, that is they provide the ability to display the data in a variety of ways, usually through multiple graphs, scaling and zooming of the graphs. However, the end-user is actually after an *interpretation* of this data, not the presentation of the data itself.

Currently, this task of interpretation is performed exclusively by the human operator. At the same time, this task of interpretation is the critical task in providing value for the entire system. Simple data collection and display has absolutely no value on its own. However, with the interpretation, it has tremendous cost and safety benefit to the particular organization.

Our work is to use expert systems in order to turn this display of data into an interpretation. Expert systems seem ideally suited for this task. Given that the data has been collected electronically and is available through electronic measurement systems, then data input and characterizing the data itself is fairly simple. At least it is well understood within the realm of industrial data acquisition.

The interpretation is performed by human operators who have a higher level of expertise among the more experienced operators than the less experienced ones. Most companies would like to retain this expertise and make it available 24 hours a day. The key maintenance personnel are usually only available for part of the day, given that they have other tasks to perform and work a standard eight hour shift. To most companies, the ability to have a consistent interpretation, 24 hours a day, tremendously increases the cost effectiveness of the overall system as well as the reliability of their machinery. By providing a lower level of necessary skill for the interpretation, companies are able to use these systems in many more situations.

Although the potential benefits seem very large, the risks inherent in the use of a new technology in a very conservative industry prevent many companies from undertaking projects of this sort. The problem of requiring people with highly skilled expert systems understanding to develop knowledge bases is a major stumbling block in such systems. The typical end-user organization does not have the time to develop an expert system; their experts are currently in such demand that diverting them to build a system is out of the question. At the same time, the technology is not considered adequately proven for industrial use, so the management is reluctant to invest several hundred thousand pounds in a project.

We have been developing systems for two primary areas of industrial data acquisition; monitoring process control systems and condition monitoring of rotating machinery.

To monitor a process control system, the first task is to acquire the process measurements. Generally, data are easily represented through dials and gauges such as the various temperatures, flow rates and power settings. These data provide a summary similar to that available from a process panel. By looking at the combination of information it is possible to determine whether the process is being run in the optimal way. If a failure has occurred, it is also possible to rapidly diagnose a fault and assist the operator in getting the plant running again. For the project described here, the plant to be monitored was a pilot plant to be used in developing better recipes.

In rotating machinery, the condition of the machine must be determined in order to identify any failures prior to their occurrence. By looking at the vibration of the bearings in the main shaft of a large pump or compressor, it is possible to detect early symptoms of any bearing failures, misalignment of the shaft, looseness of the machine or unbalance of the main rotor. Good condition monitoring enables unexpected failures to be prevented and very economical condition-based maintenance, rather than calendar-based maintenance to be performed. By fixing machinery only when it is about to break, rather than on a regular basis regardless of its condition, companies can realize tremendous cost savings and increases in process efficiency.

In this chapter we describe the system for use with a routine monitoring package. In a typical application the end-user uses a hand-held data collection device to record the vibration. A PC contains a database of the vibration signatures of all the machines as well as the time scales for checking their condition. On a daily basis an engineer will travel a route visiting a large number of machines recording the appropriate data from the bearings and housing of each machine. When he returns to the PC, the system automatically transfers the data stored in the data collector to the PC database. The software will automatically identify points in alarm, that is, points for which the vibration level exceeds some pre-set limit. The end-user requires up to four hours of manual analysis to determine what the actual problem is for each point in alarm. This analysis also requires a good understanding of machinery vibration characteristics. The system we have developed performs the same analysis automatically in only five minutes, using the expert system to diagnose the particular problems.

Both projects are actually a composite of a number of efforts made between 1986 and 1988. In fact these two projects do not represent two real projects, but actually a composite of much effort in the two different areas.

Although process control is widely considered an interesting area of activity for expert systems with a large number of projects in progress, our conclusions are that this is a very poor area for the application of expert systems, when the goal is a near-term success and a relatively easy development. The reasons for this are not due to the limitations of expert systems technology, but the type of environment and the changing characteristics of the two application areas. The data acquisition and process control systems tend to be very diverse across industry. The scale of many process monitoring systems requires a heavy initial investment in powerful hardware to handle the necessary speeds and large number of inputs. The vibration packages are bounded by the IBM PC hardware and software, and do not provide problems of time or speed.

More importantly however, the key lesson of this chapter is that the ease of building a standard knowledge base, or more importantly, the ability to deliver a system for which the end-user does not write a knowledge base, is a critical factor in how widespread these systems can become. In process monitoring we argue that it is not possible to develop a standard knowledge base for use in a system. However, in vibration monitoring, it is very practical. In fact it has been accomplished to develop one knowledge base covering the majority of machines and faults. The result is that for vibration monitoring it is possible to deliver a system to end-users where no knowledge base has been developed. However, in process control it is necessary to develop a unique knowledge base for every application. This restricts, by an order of magnitude, the number of applications which are practicable and can be deployed in the near term.

SYSTEM SPECIFICATION

In both systems, a *concept* was initially sold to the purchasing organization. This concept described the benefits and capabilities of the system that could be developed. The term concept is used to reflect that it was a very general description of benefits that could be derived and a functionality that should be possible to develop. In the process monitoring example, the expert was familiar with expert systems and

IF
THE *OUTPUT PUMP*
 IS ON
AND
THE *OUTPUT FLOW RATE*
 IS VERY LOW
AND
THE *REACTOR TEMP*
 IS HIGH

THEN
THE SUBSTANCE
HAS CONGEALED

Figure 6.1 A typical process monitoring rule

able to illustrate a number of example rules. It was also possible to identify the data that should be available and the standard hardware on which the system could be developed. From this high level briefing specification, more detailed project funding was assembled. The exact specification of the project then evolved through the development.

For the machinery monitoring system, the task which a user had to conduct was clearly understood because of the wide experience in this area. The knowledge was readily identifiable from a number of manuals and from experiences of several machinery diagnostics. In this case, the concept of the solution was sold, the more detailed specification of the project never actually existed until near the final stages.

More importantly, the specification was driven by the expectations of the potential users. If one is delivering a monitoring and diagnostic expert system, then one must provide the end-user with what the end-user believes it to mean.

In the process monitoring example the end-user group was very small, being confined to the process engineers at one factory. As a result, it was possible to discuss with the process engineers precisely what the system

ANNIE

from

Intelligent Applications Limited

PRESENT ENGINE CONDITION IS TURBINE NOZZLES BLOCKED

SUPERCHARGER PRESSURE IS	LOW	0.53	Bars
TEMPERATURE BEFORE AIR COOLER IS	NORMAL	175.43	Celsius
TEMPERATURE AFTER AIR COOLER IS	LOW	47.95	Celsius
AIR FUEL RATIO IS	LOW	12.93	
EXHAUST MANIFOLD PRESSURE IS	LOW	0.52	Bars
TEMPERATURE BEFORE TURBINE IS	HIGH	816.22	Celsius
TURBINE SPEED IS	NORMAL	21988.00	RPM
TEMPERATURE AFTER TURBINE IS	HIGH	507.89	Celsius

Press <CR> to return to Annie main menu.

Figure 6.2 The end user display for the process monitoring system (Copyright © Intelligent Applications Ltd, 1987)

would and would not do. It was also possible to receive feedback from the process engineers as to what the system must essentially do and what constraints there would be on the performance of the system. As this was one small focussed application being custom developed for a specific group of users, the process system that resulted was very close to the general expectations of a user.

In the machinery monitoring example however, the potential user base is a very large number of people with very diverse backgrounds and expectations. It was not possible to judge ahead of time what a machinery diagnostic system meant to many of the potential users. After the developers had made the system do what they thought it should, it was then shown to a large number of potential users. Each of these had a number of suggestions and comments because their *naive expectation* of what the system would do was different from its actual performance. Probably the greatest effort went into modifying and improving the functionality of the system to meet these expectations of the end-users. It is important to realize that the potential end-users never look at the specification or the agreed limitations of the system. They had a pre-conceived notion of what it should do, and that was exactly what it must do.

A FEW FAILURES

One of the key aspects of the process monitoring system is the data acquisition element itself. In an earlier stage of the process monitoring project, we attempted to gather data directly from the process plant. A reasonable budget was allocated for the rapid data acquisition of many key parameters. After two man-months of work and the consumption of the allocated budget, the system was still not nearly functional. It had now become clear that other parameters were required for the system to be effective and a considerable increase in cost would be necessary. At that stage, the management was not willing to carry on with the greater investment and risk, and so the project temporarily ground to a halt. This difficulty arose because no-one knew exactly what was needed to solve the problem, or what data items were essential in diagnosing faults in the process. The only way to understand this more clearly was to actually develop a prototype. When the amount of work became clear, there was great dismay at the funding organization, and the project was nearly abandoned. It was finally recognized that no-one had enough knowledge of the problem or its details to minimize the risks and make an accurate cost estimate. This phase of the project had nothing at all to do with the expert systems element, but was a necessary step forward. Since the end-user organization did not have an adequate understanding of the mechanical working of the process, this problem was inevitable.

An early version of the vibration monitoring system was developed for helicopter rotor blade vibration. In this system, a vibration recorder was fitted permanently into the helicopter. The pilot was able to make an analogue tape recording of the vibration at any time during the flight. Once the helicopter returned to its base, the tape was then played through a spectrum analyser, and the expert system was used to analyse the overall health of the helicopter. The system was able to provide vibration monitoring analysis at a time when nothing else was available for in-flight monitoring of the helicopter. Given several helicopter crashes and considerable loss of life in the North Sea, this would seem to be a very important step forward.

The entire project failed completely for three primary reasons. In order for the system to work, a tape recorder certified for use in-flight and for safety applications needed to be made available. Although there are a wide range of industrial vibration tape recorders, only one had the appropriate approval from the Civil Aviation Authority (CAA). The small company which produced these did not have adequate industrial resources to develop the system and promote it on a wide basis. The third problem also greatly impacted the tape recorder's availability.

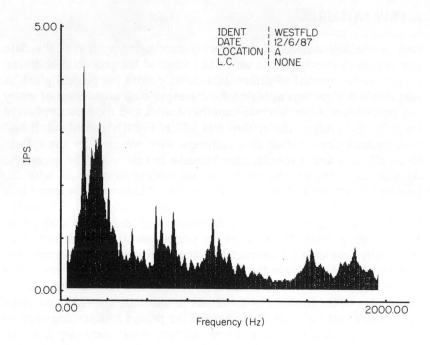

Figure 6.3   A typical vibration spectrum as the input to the diagnosis

The second difficulty was that the CAA decided not to go for a partial solution to a critical problem. The experts of helicopter systems recognize that this is only partially accurate and a partial solution. The basic problem was far more difficult and would require considerable research. Rather than accept an incremental and limited solution for a problem which had no other alternative, the decision was taken to develop a very large and powerful system over a period of several years. All the parties in the United Kingdom that could have participated and benefited from such a tape-based vibration system, instead began a massive three year program of data collection and understanding of the problems of helicopter vibration. As a result, for political reasons, this partial solution was abandoned until a completely satisfactory total solution was available.

The final problem was very much one of business logistics. The company supplying the tape recorders was only able to make a small amount of money from each tape recorder. The number of helicopters in the world was not very large, so the company would not be able to generate several million in revenue from tape recorder sales per year. Our vibration diagnosis expert system made it possible for the end-user to do the complete analysis automatically. The company supplying the tape recorders realized that the analysis of the data was a very lucrative business area for them and that our system would completely remove that revenue stream. On the other hand, the helicopter operators were not comfortable sending their tapes for analysis by another group. As there was no single supplier able to offer a total solution and generate sufficient revenues, the entire project fell apart.

USE OF RESOURCES

Both systems were designed to run on low cost standard hardware platforms that would integrate well into the existing environment. In both cases the IBM PC was selected with the C language being used for any interfaces to low level data acquisition systems and databases. The standard expert system shell Crystal was used for the rulebase and expert system element. The exact features of the elements of the system were not analysed against the problem and the characteristics or difficulty of the problem. Instead, these tools were selected as the only logical options meeting the requirements of full integration, standard hardware, and ease of use. It is our belief that the minor differences and limitations between many of the products can be overcome by highly qualified programmers. At the same time these limitations will not affect the success or failure of the project, rather the organizational and knowledge engineering issues will.

For the process monitoring system the current data acquisition system is a Texas Instruments process control computer. Communications between the expert system on the PC and the process control computer was via an RS232 serial interface. The protocol of communications is the standard X-MODEM protocol, selected because of its wide usage. The cost of the PC and software was well under £10 000. However, the cost of integrating the serial communications, testing and proving it was in excess of £40 000. In order to implement the expert system it was necessary to gain the support and cooperation of the process control software development group. Although they were generally receptive to the idea, a major problem was caused when they realized this was a serious project and that they would actually have to let someone interface to their computer. As a result, a project that seemed guaranteed suddenly ground to a halt for 2 months while management was involved in getting further support for providing the interface. As a different group was in charge of process control software, a high level of management had to be involved.

Once support was received, the software development and testing of the protocol on the process control computer had to be carried out by the process control group themselves. This group of people acted as a computer support group to the rest of the company, but were very overworked. In order to develop the interface software they then had to produce a specification and in excess of 2 man-months of work to implement the communications protocol. Testing and implementation of it required further work. This generated tremendous problems since the process control computer was busy with the process itself and little time was available for actual testing.

Since the system we were supplying had to communicate with their computer, the logistics of getting together the developers, the end-users and the process control team for systems tasks proved very difficult and further delays in scheduling were introduced into the project.

After the communications had been working for several months, further problems were discovered, i.e. certain memory problems would occur after the system had been running for 15 hours continuously. In other situations, the odd data item would be missed out in the communications. It became virtually impossible to debug such problems over long-distance communications and by communicating with the end-user as well as the process control team. Two years later, some of these bugs still exist in the software. More time has been consumed for the support of the communications link and debugging it than the original software project development.

The speed of the Crystal expert system shell meant that no speed limitations were encountered. At the end of this project, we had a slightly flaky serial communications interface to one specific process control computer. In order to replicate this system on other installations, the same amount of work again will be necessary to implement another communications protocol and do further debugging tests. The communications has represented a significant investment as part of the total project, although the experience will accelerate the next project.

This experience contrasts completely with that of the rotating machinery diagnostic system. In this case a database in dBase II format was available on-line on the IBM PC computer. Documents were obtained describing the exact database structure. Approximately one man-month of work was spent in the initial development of an interface to read the database structures and convert those into the internal C routines needed for the Violet software. A further man-month of work was spent testing and debugging this and making minor improvements for robustness and loading up more detailed information. Now that the interface has been written, it is directly transferable to over a thousand different customers with the same system. In addition this proved a useful building block to write an interface to a similar database from another supplier. We were able to greatly leverage the time and experience gained in the first project for other projects. The testing phase was far simpler and the resulting system worked extremely well.

The differences in integration between these two are fundamental to the different problem tasks, their ease and success. In process control the interfacing task was extremely complex and unique to particular customers' requirements. It necessitated involving a third party of programmers, i.e. the process control people themselves. This greatly increased the complexity and cost of the project.

In the rotating machinery example, the database was fairly simple and straightforward, it did not require another group and was done very quickly. The resulting project has high repetitive leverage. This means that the resulting system is much more cost-effective and much easier to replicate widely.

The staffing involved in both projects was very similar. In general, competent IBM PC programmers were used, with the author as the expert systems expert. All the low-level interfacing and database accessing was done by programmers who knew the IBM PC and C programming well, but very little about expert systems.

In the process monitoring system the end-user was actually a member of the expert system group for that company. He had an extensive background in process control and attended a number of expert systems courses. He developed the expert system rulebase himself.

In the machinery example, the author worked with one of the machinery experts from the machinery acquisition company to develop a very robust and powerful system. The machinery expert was able to write his own rules in Crystal after just a few hours of examples. Although he was able to write rules very quickly, these rules still required cleaning up and restructuring by someone more experienced in the expert systems methodology. In general, the rulebase reflects not only pure facts and domain specific knowledge, but they also have to be structured in a way to make the analysis of the problem work more appropriately. For example, being able to loop repetitively over some sections of the rulebase and being able to find all possible rules that match, requires special techniques. Although these techniques were fairly simple, the beginner will tend to structure rules in such a way that it can be very difficult to implement them.

The rulebases in both cases required several man-months of work. This categorizes them as non-trivial systems, they all had several hundred rules, but they were also not exceptionally complex. In both cases a general specification of the project had been developed before it had started.

As a prototype was developed and evolved, the final specification was fine-tuned and evolved in parallel. As both projects broke new ground in terms of the capabilities with which they provided the end-user it was not possible to accurately estimate ahead of time exactly what the solution should look like. During the development each project was managed in order to determine how best to add to the capability and functionality. Specifications were in general finalized and improved in detail after the basis system had been developed. The usage of IBM PC hardware meant that development and delivery environments were the same in both cases.

INVOLVEMENT OF USERS

Initially it was expected that the users would be deeply involved in the project. They were informed at the start of the project of the rough goals and direction of the project. They had some general input to the development of the project, but the end-users were scarcely involved. The primary reason for not involving the end-users at an early stage was the fact that they had many other tasks to perform and did not completely understand the concept of the expert system being developed. The systems were intended to be simple to use and solve a complete problem, so the performance details and what steps it went through were not actually critical to the end-user.

However, it was critical that the end-user found the system usable and so extensive discussions about the user interface were conducted.

In the process monitoring project, the person developing the rulebase was himself a process engineer and developed a good rapport with the end-users. We, as system providers, were not involved at all with the end-user.

In the rotating machinery example we relied on the knowledge of the machinery expert and his understanding of the customer base. Various presentations were made to prospective end-users, and feedback was received about their concerns on what the system had to do. These inputs were often from an attempted sale of the early developed version of the system, but did provide valuable guidance on the capabilities of the resulting system. In order to ensure that the end-users did not become disenchanted with the system, they were not exposed to it until we were happy that the systems test and final test efforts had been completed. The problem that the system is solving is critical to their own functionality, thus end-user acceptance was relatively easy to obtain. This is one area where the end-user was not involved to the extent that normally would have been expected. This was not a major problem in this system because it was dominated by many of the other issues, such as the integration and development of the knowledge base.

KNOWLEDGE ACQUISITION

Of the two example systems, the author was involved in the rulebase development of only one of the systems. In the process monitoring system, only the process engineer knew enough about the process to develop the knowledge base. Fortunately, this person was also trained in expert systems and as a result the knowledge base was developed from his own personal experience. His experience was then tested against raw data, and discussed with the process engineers until it was fine-tuned to a working system.

For the machinery monitoring example, the author worked in partnership with one of the world's experts on rotating machinery diagnosis. The knowledge base development was focussed by discussing the types of machine for which the knowledge base should be applied. For this group of machines, a list was also made of the common faults with which the knowledge base should deal. For each fault, the manner of manifestation and identification was then discussed. The author learned very quickly how to perform the diagnosis himself. As a result, he was able to write many of the rules directly in the system. At the same time, the machinery expert rapidly learned how to use the expert system shell. After only one day of joint knowledge base development, the expert would typically spend several hours writing more rules to cover larger classes of fault. The author would then edit and restructure the rules so that they were cleaned up. As the resulting rulebase was run on more and more examples, inconsistencies or gaps in the rulebase were discovered and rules were developed to cover these faults.

We feel it is important that no method of interviewing or protocol analysis was used through the capability of rapid prototype, two people worked in close partnership educating the other on the appropriate skills.

REPRESENTATION AND REASONING

The systems were both developed on the IBM PC and the basic approach to representation and reasoning was similar. When analysing and contrasting the success or failure of a project, the fact that these are constant helps to show that this is not a critical detail. Both systems used very simple knowledge representation, the state of the system was described by a number of parameters such as the value of various pressures, temperatures, flow rates or the value of various vibration levels such as harmonics, blade pass frequencies, gear mesh frequencies or ball bearing frequencies. All of the data values were simple parameter-value combinations. This resulted in a very simple knowledge representation mechanism.

Both systems used the Crystal expert system shell, which is a pure backward chaining rule-based system. Neither system had any fundamental problems with this type of reasoning mechanism. The control structure was the straightforward backward chaining structure of the system. However, it was necessary to implement various mechanisms for causing rules to fail explicitly in order that it had the correct behaviour for dealing with exclusive sets of problems or combinations of problems. In general, we would always make the system find all possible rules that match. To accomplish this, the behaviour of the backward chaining system was altered, such that it found all rules rather than stopping on the first rule. This is done by putting a FAIL at the end of every rule so the system believes that no rules have succeeded. All rules or conclusions displayed were done then as side effects of the rule matching process. Strictly speaking, this is not how the rules should be developed, but was a very efficient mechanism.

In both systems, uncertainty was not dealt with. It is the belief of the author that when you run out of knowledge you start to use numbers. It would make no sense to put probabilities that were arbitrary and ill-understood on the rotating machinery diagnostic system. The rules are all of the form, 'if this rule matches then symptoms of this fault do definitely exist'. Ranking how severe the problems are or how likely they were relative to each other was just not appropriate. The rulebases were oriented around discovering 'does this problem exist or not', thus the probability or fuzzy set comparisons were not relevant. The data acquisition provided definite values that were quantitative in nature and so human judgement fields were not necessary. In general, the rules were based on fundamental engineering principles so attenuation factors similar to Mycin were not needed.

Both rule bases were fairly similar in size, having approximately three hundred rules, of which one hundred and fifty were used in the control and organization of the system, and one hundred and fifty were used for the actual diagnostic position of the system. The machinery diagnostic system has almost four hundred C access routine calls for the low level interaction. Both systems also used about one hundred variables to store intermediate values and conclusions.

USER INTERFACE

In both systems, the user interface was simple and straightforward. It was developed exclusively using the capabilities of the Crystal expert system shell. Although this provides nice graphics and displays, it does not provide a more complicated multi-interaction system. For example, mouse input or multiple windows were not used. In the rotating machinery system, the number of screens the end-users see was greatly restricted to make it as easy to use as possible, with the resulting total of twelve different output displays available. These displays included several 'yes', 'no' questions, a few title and introductory slides, a number of options to pick the type of analysis and a group of machines to analyse. There was no elaborate user interface mechanism used, no user model, multi-video systems were involved. In some cases, EGA graphics screens were considered, but were not considered to contribute to the value of the system to justify their extra cost.

We feel it very important that in these systems the user interface, knowledge representation and control mechanisms were standard as provided by a standard product. No further development time was consumed for these areas.

EVALUATION

A precise evaluation of either project is very difficult. The initial objectives and desires were vague at the best, it was hoped that some benefit would derive from the system, and if this could be spotted in the final implementation, then that would prove an adequate method. The evaluation was provided in two main sections, whether the system actually performed the task adequately and whether that provided adequate benefits.

The machinery monitoring system was tested on a large number of machinery databases. Data for every fault was identified and the system was tested to be certain that every fault did occur. For several large databases, the system was also checked to make sure that the diagnosis it developed was the same as a human expert would have developed. As many combinations of user options and data examples were used as possible to make sure that the system was robust. In the early stages, a number of major faults were discovered. Some were as radical as causing the entire screen contents of the PC to be sent to the printer non-stop, others were minor bugs that would probably never have caused a fault, but in theory could have.

The primary goal of the system was to have an accurate and rapid diagnosis. The accuracy was checked by considering a large number of case examples. The speed was such a dramatic improvement over previous systems that no formal detailed analysis was required. As the process monitoring system could run very quickly on an easily controllable database, it was possible to conduct a thorough test of the system.

For the process monitoring system, most of the evaluation was focussed on whether the system was actually able to perform the task in a continuous and accurate manner. Test data were supplied through prepared simulation data files. It was not possible to have the plant generate every failure for real, as this would cause considerable havoc. As long as the system seemed to be working properly and responded properly to the simulation data, it was taken to be working effectively.

At the time of writing, both projects are still in their early stages of usage and detailed evaluations are not available.

Although there was a strong desire to write a detailed test specification for both projects, this occurred in neither project. The resulting complexity of the system and the time scales for development precluded this exhaustive testing. In practice, both systems are working effectively.

ORGANIZATIONAL ISSUES

The organizational issues were the dominating factors on the success and failures of all the projects we have been involved with. As will be clear from the previous sections, the technical aspects of knowledge representation, user interface, uncertainty and knowledge engineering were kept to a very simple minimum. In this way, there was no great technical challenge in any of the projects, thus it was much easier to understand the impact of the organizational issues. The data acquisition system was a major element in this style of on-line system. The primary difficulty with the data acquisition, however, was not the technical aspects, but the managerial aspects. In order to provide a link between the expert system and the existing process systems, it is necessary to have managerial support at the highest levels. This support had to provide justification to the process department for it to provide access to their information and computer from an external group. The process engineers were presented with a new interpretive capability, which at the same time greatly complemented their skills and also threatened their own jobs.

This partly represents the problem of systems integration and the fact that such projects cut across the whole organizational structure of a company. As a result, the systems integration commitment has to be considerable. This requires different management teams with different objectives all agreeing to a common high risk project. In the projects which failed as they were beginning, the organizational issues also played a major role. In the first project, the expectation of the management was not consistent with the understanding of the problem by the technical team. As a result, when the technical team developed a more detailed understanding and discovered the problem was much harder than expected, the management withdrew support for the project.

In the case of the helicopter vibration system, the methods by which a company can actually make money and the integration of these systems into company economics prevented the type of solution that was available from being financially viable, not for the end-user, but for the supplying company. As a result, a fairly simple technical solution became impossible.

The large scale and amount of risk of the process monitoring systems means that considerable management support is needed and the system crosses many different aspects of the company. By contrast the vibration monitoring project is a simple addition to the current data acquisition system. It does not require interfacing with other groups or any external support, this means that the project is very quick and simple to develop and replicate.

Although both these systems address what seem to be key problems, they are not the critical needs of a company. The process monitoring system does produce considerable cost benefit by optimizing the raw material consumption and minimizing product wastage. However, the project still needed to be considered as a strategic development investment in both examples. Without the expert system, the project or product that the end-user company produced will not be affected. Instead they helped to optimize the process. As a result, they are not absolutely needed.

We like to think that these systems are analogous to a microwave oven. No-one actually requires a microwave oven to survive. For many years every home went without a microwave oven, as a result the microwave can be considered a luxury. On the other hand, the microwave does save considerable time and is much easier to use than a traditional oven or cooking surface. As a result, once they became accepted, they spread rapidly and now it is the norm to have a microwave oven.

This can be contrasted with selling light bulbs. It is essential for every household to have light bulbs in order to provide light. As a result, the demand in the market for them is much greater and the justification for buying light bulbs is much smaller in its requirements. As it was recognized that we were selling microwaves and not light bulbs, the product justification and impact on the organization was treated very differently. It should be noted that in both projects, the management commitment was very strong. In many cases we have been exposed to potential process monitoring systems where the management commitment is not very strong. The result has been that the project did not begin in the first place.

If we think what could have been developed in process monitoring, almost all of these potential projects have failed, because there was not adequate management commitment to offset the high cost and risk. In all cases, considerable benefit was possible, but this was not enough to justify an effort.

Another major organizational problem is the lack of ability of those companies to calculate the exact return on investment. The process monitoring system helps to optimize the raw materials and prevent wastage. If one knew the actual cost of these materials, the amount lost through current wastage and the expected percentage improvement, one can easily calculate the financial benefit per year. It was discovered that no method existed for tracking and quantifying the exact amount of wastage at the current time. Wastage and inefficiency arise from a large number of sources and these were not carefully identified and tracked. As a result, it was virtually impossible to make a precise forecast of the improvements and the impact they have had. Essentially the organization did not understand in quantitative terms what its problem was, and as a result was not able to calculate the return on investment. As this return could not be calculated, the task had to be justified as a strategic one, rather than a pure investment.

In the machinery monitoring example however, the improvements are all related to time and are easy to calculate. The analysis of all of the machines with potential problems on a route will require, on average, about four hours for an experienced engineer to conduct. The system we developed is able to do the complete analysis unattended in only five minutes. Assuming full utilization of the machinery engineer, which is a valid assumption in large companies, this implies the saving of one half of a man year. There are many indirect savings, but this half man year is already at least triple the cost of the basic system. Although return on investment is the classic way to justify the sale, in general it was not possible to identify what the actual savings would be because no one knew what their exact costs were.

CONCLUSION

In this paper we have described two projects; the first was a process monitoring system using an expert system for data interpretation and the second a machinery condition diagnosis system also using an expert system for data interpretation. Although technically the systems were very similar, the commonality of the expertise required to solve the problem radically changed the cost and usefulness of the solutions.

In the process monitoring example, a non-standard rulebase was developed at a very high cost which was not easy to use for other applications. In the condition monitoring example, a low cost was required to develop a standard knowledge base which was then used in many situations.

The lessons can be summarized in Rob's 'Laws of Expert Systems Projects'.

The three basic equations are:

Volume = 1/Price
Price = Difficulty of sale
Risk = 1/Acceptable price.

These laws state some very simple facts, the higher the volume available for the resulting solution, the lower the price at which it can be produced. This implies that low volume projects have extremely high costs associated with them. In this chapter the process monitoring system was an example of a low volume product. The rotating machinery example is that of a high volume product, with resulting appropriate prices. The cost of an item radically affects how difficult it is for a company to make a purchase. It is very easy to obtain authority to purchase something for only fifty pounds. It takes a lot of work and management commitment in order to obtain a system for fifty thousand pounds. Therefore, the systems which are able to replicate in high volume and will sell at lower price, will find a ready market and be much easier for the consuming organization to be able to purchase. The low difficulty of sale reflects both the difficulty of a third party company selling to an end-user organization, and also for the end-user organization to make the buying decision and bring the product on board. The difficulty of sale is also closely coupled with the time needed to make a decision. The third law is very important, in that it is one of the dominating factors in how these systems can be evolved. In general, people are not willing to risk large amounts of funds. They are willing to spend fifty pounds on something that is not very likely to work, but unlikely to want to spend fifty thousand pounds on something that is unlikely to work. Obviously, high volume replications have a fairly low risk, but large systems projects with extensive development times are a very high risk. The risk factor means that large low volume projects are extremely difficult to justify and begin. Low volume and resulting low cost systems are very easy to justify, even if the risk is considerable, although the risk in general will be very low. Theoretically, the cost savings or return on investment should be the guiding factor on making a purchase decision. In reality, this does not seem to be a major part of the process, instead the absolute levels of cost and risk are the considerations even though large scale process monitoring systems will have considerable pay back. In general the clear high level of risk and high cost prevents companies from moving forward anyway. All this leads to the conclusion that although process control is receiving considerable interest and activity, it is doomed to grow very slowly.

Other areas where low cost systems can be developed for volume representation will benefit from tremendous growth. It is these areas on which the future spread and growth of expert systems technology and its applications to industry relies.

BIBLIOGRAPHY

Barr, A. and Feigenbaum, E. (1981). *The Handbook of Artificial Intelligence*, William Kaufman Press, California.

Clocksin, W. and Morgan, A. (1986). *Qualitative Control*, Proceedings of ECAI-86, Brighton England, July 21–25.

Harmon, P. (1986). *Expert Systems Strategies*, Cutter Information Corp. Vol 2., No. 8 August.

Kaemmerer, W. and Allard, J. (1987). *An Automated Reasoning Technique for Providing Moment-by-Moment Advice Concerning the Operation of a Process*, AAAI '87 Proceedings, Seattle, Washington, 13–17 July, Vol. 2, pp.809–813.

Mavrovouniotis, M. and Stephanopoulos, G. (1987). *Reasoning with Orders of*

Magnitude and Approximate Relations, AAAI '87 Proceedings, Seattle, Washington, 13–17 July, Vol. 2, pp.626–630.

Milne, R. (1986). Artificial Intelligence Applied to Condition Health Monitoring, *Chartered Mechanical Engineer*, 33, No.5, May 1986.

Milne, R. (1986). *Fault Diagnosis & Expert Systems*, In R. W. Milne and B. Chandrasekaran (eds.), The 6th International Workshop on Expert Systems & Their Applications, Avignon, France, 28–30 April.

Milne, R. (1987). *Diagnostics and Machine Health—On-Line Expert Systems*, Expert Systems in Process Control Seminar, London, 14th October.

Milne, R. (1987). *Artificial Intelligence for On-Line Diagnosis, IEE Proc.*, 134D, No.4, July.

Milne, R. (1987). Strategies for Diagnosis, *IEEE Transactions on Systems, Man, and Cybernetics*, SMC-17, No.3.

Milne, R. (1987). *On-Line Artificial Intelligence*, The 7th International Workshop on Expert Systems & Their Applications, Avignon, France, 13–15 May.

Milne, R. (1987). *Artificial Intelligence for Vibration Based Health Monitoring*, Fourth European Conference on Non-Destructive Testing, September, London, UK.

Milne, R. (1988). *Rapid Fault Diagnosis*. Expert Systems Industrial Hazards Conference, 31st October, The Cafe Royal, London, UK.

Milne, R. (1988). *The Role of Artificial Intelligence in Condition Monitoring and Diagnosis*. Comaden 88, 20–21st September, Birmingham, UK.

Milne, R. (1988). *Artificial Intelligence for Rotating Machinery Monitoring*. IMACS 1988 12th World Congress on Scientific Computation, July 18–22, Paris, France.

Milne, R. (1988). *Intelligent Condition Based Maintenance*, Pira, Paper & Board Division Conference, 8–10th March, Dorking, UK.

Moore, R. (1986). *Expert Systems in Process Control: Applications Experience*, First International Conference on Applications of Artificial Intelligence to Engineering Problems, Southampton, England, 15–18 April.

Winston, P. (1984). *Artificial Intelligence*, Addison-Wesley, Reading, MA.

7

RBEST: An Expert System for Disk Failure Diagnosis During Manufacturing

Keith Braunwalder and Stefek Zaba

ABSTRACT

RBEST is a system which determines the cause of failure in disk drives during their final 24 hour environmental stress test at the end of the manufacturing process. It has been in successful use since the end of 1986, and has proved crucial in allowing a 20-fold increase in the production rate of disk drives. To date it is estimated to have saved Hewlett-Packard Company at least $1M in direct labour savings alone, for a total cost of $150K.

INTRODUCTION

The RBEST project was started as an experimental application of expert

---

systems techniques at the Disk Memory Division of HP (Hewlett-Packard) in early 1986, as the division prepared for large increases in the number of disk drives to be produced in the coming years. A successful prototype was implemented in the space of three months on a strictly experimental basis by one engineer (the first-named author), who came to the project with no previous background in expert systems applications. The system has been in regular production use since late 1986. Since that time it has been incrementally reworked and enhanced, and the number of disk drives whose final test results are interpreted by the system each month has increased by more than an order of magnitude. The diagnostic accuracy of the system on those drives which do not pass a 24-hour test is now well over 99%; a more detailed performance analysis is given later. The system has also proved invaluable in tracking failure trends: since the categorization of failures is stable and repeatable, changes from the previous pattern of failures are meaningful indicators of improvements or degradations.

The initial motivation for the RBEST prototype was to investigate whether the research promise of expert systems techniques (Feigenbaum and McCorduck 1984) could be applied in practice to assist in scaling up the production of disk drives at DMD, with the production increases foreseen as HP sold more workstation computers and increased its presence in the OEM disk mechanism market.

A bottleneck in the production process which was rapidly identified and seemed to be squarely in the mould of problems successfully tackled by previously reported expert systems was the interpretation of the results of the final 24 hour environmental and electrical stress testing of disk drives. The drives which passed this test could be shipped with high confidence; the failing drives, however, represented a significant inventory cost, and the identification of the precise cause of the reported faults from the failure printout (which ranged from a few cryptic lines to 17 or more pages of detailed low-level parametric data) was time-consuming and error-prone.

A particularly costly and too frequent event was the transfer of a drive to 'debug technicians' after some inconclusive attempts at diagnosis by the operator supervising the test. The debug technician would attempt to reproduce the fault, run extensive tests on sub-assemblies, possibly exchange some components, and finally return the drive for final test with 'No Fault Found'—at which point the drive might fail again, and this time be rapidly fixed by a different technician or engineer. Such cycling of 'No Fault Found' drives proved to be a large waste of time and manpower.

```
+----------------------------------------------------------------------+
|   --------------------------------- 14.0 -------------------------    |
|   HEAD     0     S O F T   D I S C   E R R O R S   ( C A T   1 )      |
|   ----------------------------------------------------------------    |
|   S L   L  L  D  Byt                        Status  One One Rm  Er Test|
|   P Cyl Hd Sec Sec Num Data Read  ErrMsk     Byte   Occ Lth Tmp Id Stp |
|   ----------------------------------------------------------------    |
|      195  0  27  26  1     000000 FFFFFF 0     r     48  48  2C  EC  66 |
|      195  0  30  29  1     000000 FFFFFF H     r     48  48 -5C  EC  66 |
|      195  0  36  35  1     000000 FFFFFF 0     r     48  48 -5C  EC  66 |
|      195  0  40  39  1     000000 FFFFFF H     r     48  48 -5C  EC  66 |
|      195  0  44  43 99 DB6DB5AC02 03776F . B   r    255 255 -5C  EC  66 |
|      195  0  47  46  1     000000 FFFFFF H     r     48  48 -5C  EC  66 |
|      195  0  55  54 59 B6DB21000C 4CB6D7   B   r    255 255 -5C  EC  66 |
|   ----------------------------------------------------------------    |
|   Errors Printed =     7                                              |
|   ----------------------------------------------------------------    |
|                                                                      |
+----------------------------------------------------------------------+
```

Figure 7.1 A small fragment of the raw data input to RBEST—the test report produced on each drive. The report from which this fragment is culled runs to over 3000 lines of printout

OBJECTIVES

The initial objective of the project was to investigate the utility of expert systems technology. The area chosen for experimentation with expert systems techniques was the interpretation of the results of the final 24-hour environmental and electrical stress testing of disk drives. As the experiment progressed through successive rounds of prototyping, the objectives changed from an evaluation of the general potential of the technology to much more specific ones relating to the specific testing process. These more specific objectives included:

* less time spent on diagnosing and fixing each failing drive
* successful fix implemented more often by less skilled people
* fewer 'no fault found' units resubmitted for test with no satisfactory explanation of failure.

As implementation of the system progressed further and the feasibility of meeting these objectives was established, more precise numerical measures were established for them, and additional objectives relating to the system itself were added:

* coverage: initially 98%, and now 100% of all failing drives to receive a diagnostic report from RBEST

* accuracy: initially 90%, and now 98% of drives fixed by recommended action. (This objective is more complex to state in full, because of the two classes of users of the system's output— test operators on the one hand, and the more experienced debug technicians and debug engineers on the other. The section on system specification contains more information on these classes of users; the section on evaluation discusses performance measurements in more detail.)

Direct financial benefit has only recently entered into the assessment of RBEST's performance. As for many process improvements (be they expert-system assisted or not), the return-on-investment calculation is unclear, particularly ahead of implementation, since quality improvements bring large indirect benefits whose dollar impact can be

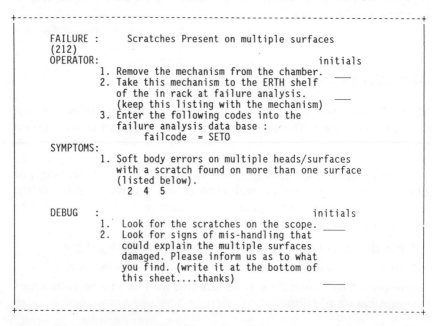

```
+--------------------------------------------------------------------+
|                                                                    |
|       FAILURE :      Scratches Present on multiple surfaces        |
|       (212)                                                        |
|       OPERATOR:                                         initials   |
|              1. Remove the mechanism from the chamber.     ___     |
|              2. Take this mechanism to the ERTH shelf              |
|                 of the in rack at failure analysis.        ___     |
|                 (keep this listing with the mechanism)            |
|              3. Enter the following codes into the                |
|                 failure analysis data base :                      |
|                       failcode = SETO                             |
|       SYMPTOMS:                                                    |
|              1. Soft body errors on multiple heads/surfaces       |
|                 with a scratch found on more than one surface     |
|                 (listed below).                                   |
|                 2  4  5                                           |
|                                                                    |
|       DEBUG   :                                         initials   |
|              1. Look for the scratches on the scope.      ___     |
|              2. Look for signs of mis-handling that               |
|                 could explain the multiple surfaces               |
|                 damaged. Please inform us as to what              |
|                 you find. (write it at the bottom of              |
|                 this sheet....thanks)                     ___     |
|                                                                    |
+--------------------------------------------------------------------+
```

Figure 7.2 RBEST sample output. A printed report containing these four sections (type of failure, instructions to test operator, symptoms pointing to the type of fault, and repair/analysis hints to the technician or engineer who will fix the fault) is produced for each failing drive. Situations recoverable by the operator alone result in reports containing only the first three sections

tweaked by at least one order of magnitude according to the motivations of those doing the ROI analysis! The figure of $1 million to date is certainly conservative; further analysis is given in the section on evaluation.

SYSTEM SPECIFICATION

Context

The RBEST system is used at the final test stage of the manufacturing process. The major subassemblies are separately tested prior to their incorporation in the product; however, this final stage tests the entire collection of components, and tests the interaction and correct combination of the pretested sub-assemblies. Additionally, the final test submits the whole unit to extremes of temperature, humidity, and supply voltage beyond the specified range of use, so stressing any marginal components into revealing malfunctions which might otherwise occur at a later date when in use by the customer.

The test is administered under the control of a Hewlett-Packard series 1000 industrial automation computer. A suite of Fortran programs controls the environment within the chamber, and performs a predetermined series of tests (read/write, servo, etc.) on each of the several hundred drives which are in the chamber at any one time. Before the introduction of RBEST, a test report for each failing drive was printed by this suite of Fortran programs. As can be seen in Figure 7.1, this output relates entirely to the surface symptoms of the failure, showing the test parameters in effect at time of failure (data being read/written, disk address, test elapsed time, temperature, humidity, supply voltage and so on). It turns out that what is important in relating this output to the likely cause of test failure (and hence to repair action) is a combination of higher-level patterns within one section of the failure report, and the correlation of failures with various environmental or disk-geometry factors. The report printed by the Fortran programs offers no assistance with such interpretation.

Three groups of people are primarily concerned with individual disk drive failures. The first is test operators, who have a detailed knowledge of the testing procedure, and of the frequent trivial causes of test failure, such as faulty connections to the unit under test, but who usually have limited knowledge about the design or intended function of the disk drives. The information on the failing unit available to the operator before the introduction of RBEST was essentially limited to the printed output from the test control program. Few operators were able to recognize, on the basis of that printout alone, the difference between a serious failure requiring repair of the drive and a trivial failure such as a loose connection of the cable to the unit under test.

The second group is debug technicians: they have varying degrees of experience with and success in determining the cause of failure from the printout of the test control program, though all received product-specific training in this task. They have access to extensive test equipment which is able to probe internal signals within the unit, to additional diagnostic programs, and to 'known good' drives and sub-assemblies which can be used for comparison and swapping purposes.

The third group is debug engineers, some of whom will have been involved in designing the product now under manufacture. They deal with failures in a number of different products, and are expected to cope with more or less arbitrarily complex failures. Their intended role is less that of 'expert fixer' in support of the debug technicians, but more to identify the root cause of the failures, and take action to improve the manufacturing process so as to eliminate that class of failure altogether. In practice, a good deal of their time before the introduction of RBEST was spent in reviewing the output of the test control program to assist the technicians in correctly identifying the failure codes for the failure tracking database and starting them on the correct diagnosis path.

Before the introduction of RBEST, then, it was common for drives to be fixed and diagnosed by people unnecessarily far along the diagnosis route: this meant that both debug technicians and debug engineers were swamped with 'trivial' (to them) fixes, whilst the test operators and debug technicians were unable to contribute as fully to the process as they might, for the want of 'just a little' knowledge. In addition, it was not uncommon that in the presence of multiple deviations from desired behaviour, both engineers and technicians would concentrate on the most significant deviation and miss the secondary symptoms, causing the drive to fail again after a 'repair' action had been taken appropriate to repairing the primary problem alone.

Production and evolution of the system specification

The context as described above seemed to provide an auspicious opportunity for a fair test of expert systems techniques. Expertise was available—some of the operators, technicians and engineers were very competent at diagnosis, and the potential pay-off in improving the efficiency of the testing process and feeding its results more systematically into the continuous quality improvement programme was clear.

The initial, relatively informal system specification was produced by the investigating engineer after a short feasibility assessment. This first prototype aimed to diagnose (that is, correctly identify corrective action for) 90-odd per cent of the failures occurring on a well established, low-volume disk drive. This initial evaluation criterion was felt to be equivalent to the diagnostic competence of a good diagnostic technician; meeting this level of performance within the time and effort budget would show the utility of expert systems technology. As the viability of the approach became more certain, more stringent and ambitious coverage and correctness targets were established, as outlined in the sections on objectives and evaluation. Fortunately, the overall context for the system stayed stable throughout the evolutionary prototyping phases.

USE OF RESOURCES

Hardware and software environment, selection, and integration

The test controller, as described above, is an HP1000 industrial automation computer. In developing RBEST, this was a fixed part of the context: it was neither feasible nor desirable to replace this test control machine during the experimental development; on the other hand, it was not feasible to develop the expert system on that computer—aside from the lack of existing ES tools, adding an unproven and potentially resource-hungry software component to the existing system would not have proved popular! It was, therefore, decided to download the textual output which was currently being interpreted by the test operators and debug technicians to a remote machine, for analysis by the RBEST system. The link is a simple file transfer using standard local-area networking between the HP1000 system and the RBEST host machine; this required minimal modification to the HP1000 test control software.

The machine chosen as host for the RBEST system itself was the HP9000 series 300, a Motorola 680x0-based workstation running HP-UX. The choice was motivated by the availability of both 'conventional' and AI software, the latter being (at the time of prototyping) HP's proprietary LISP environment and a simple MYCIN-like shell. This environment offered more than enough performance for prototyping experiments without excessive concern for CPU usage, and a degree of support in the use of the environment was available from HP corporate bodies. This hardware also has entirely adequate performance to be used as the delivery vehicle: one of the smaller machines in the range is used as the delivery engine, while enhancement and regression testing is carried out on a larger, separate workstation.

Staffing

The project was started on the initiative of the first-named author, Keith Braunwalder, who brought enthusiasm and a general software background to the project but no previous experience of expert systems development (or indeed of disk diagnosis). Keith attended a three-week intensive AI technology course at HP's Corporate Engineering facility in Palo Alto: this course focussed on various AI programming techniques (rule-based, frame-based, and so on), with limited information on the practical application of these techniques, or on techniques for acquiring domain knowledge. He also received a degree of support from HP's longer-term AI research effort, both in using the environment and later in identifying deeper structure in the rulebase to make maintenance easier.

The prototype stage was staffed by Keith alone, with active support from his immediate boss, who not only supervised the development of the system but acted as a management 'champion', isolating him from potential pressures due to unrealistic expectations of the prototype's initial functionality. As the system progressed through the rounds of prototyping described in the following sub-section and came into regular production use, a second engineer was added to the team, and has concentrated on 'perfective' maintenance, such as enhancing performance and modifying the output format for clarity. Keith has concentrated on 'adaptive' maintenance (updating the rulebase to reflect new classes of failure and changes in the relative frequency of different causes of given symptoms) and on investigations of new systems broadly similar to RBEST.

Design method

The design method used was one of iterated prototyping, where each stage of prototyping had visible deliverables and resolved a particular area of uncertainty identified in the feasibility investigation. These frequent checkpoints also provided demonstrable progress, important both to sustain the interest of the experts providing the critical knowledge, and to reassure management that some return was likely on the investment of effort.

The key deliverables from each phase were:

1. 'Question and Answer Toy'
   This established the basic tractability of the domain for rule-based diagnosis: the domain expert sat down at the computer and answered questions about the presence or absence of particular patterns on the test control system's report about a drive, and was given a simple diagnosis when enough questions had been asked.
2. Batch Data
   This established the feasibility of a system operating on its own, directly from the printed data, without an intervening expert to answer questions about patterns in the input data. At this stage, the data had to be loaded manually: initially by tape, and then by a direct link to the HP1000 controller, but not yet in 'real time'.
3. Integrated System
   This established a totally automatic and responsive data transfer and diagnosis route: the system ran for a few weeks with over 75% accuracy. This was sufficiently high to excite even the sceptics!
4. Pilot Run
   This established that the initial coverage and accuracy goals for the system had been met (in fact, exceeded). Close scrutiny of the system's diagnostic accuracy over a period of three weeks—well over the 90% target—was sufficient to convince local management that the RBEST system was 'real'.

After this successful prototype, RBEST was put into production use, with its architecture essentially unchanged to this day, and gradual refinement of the content of the rulebase as further experience was gained.

INVOLVEMENT OF USERS

During the investigation phase, several expert systems were investigated, from the viewpoint of both the system designers and the targeted users. It seemed that the designers and users saw each system in a totally different light. The designers spoke of how accurate the system was, while the users spoke exclusively of their interaction with the system. The users typically had one of two concerns: either they were not comfortable with a computer (which might be overcome with training), or they complained that the same 'preliminary' questions were always asked by the system. This tedium often discouraged the users from using the system.

The designers were right about the accuracy of their systems; the knowledge bases were very concise and drew very accurate conclusions. The users were also correct: they had not really been considered during the design of the system. In looking at the needs of RBEST's intended users, one thing was clear: the test operators would have neither the time nor the inclination to manually answer questions about the printed output from the Fortran test control suite. Indeed, to answer those questions accurately required precisely the skill in interpretation of the test results which the expert system was supposed to make more widely available. This reinforced the desire to have RBEST directly parse the test output, and present its diagnostic and repair recommendations on paper.

Both groups of users were then (and still are) closely involved in the design of the printed output from the RBEST system. As can be seen in Figure 7.2 and is discussed in more detail later, the chosen output format has a detailed sequence of repair actions, and a check that these actions have indeed resolved the failure. Of the two sets of users, the test operators find that the output is now essentially stable and satisfactory: the debug technicians and engineers find that the structure and overall content are satisfactory, but that following the precise sequence of recommended tests and actions does not always result in the fastest resolution of the problem.

An integral part of the production use of RBEST in which its users play a continuing role is the monitoring of its accuracy. Space is provided on each diagnostic report to record whether the actions recommended resolved the failure, and to provide any additional comments. This information is used to keep the rulebase up to date.

KNOWLEDGE ACQUISITION

Knowledge acquisition was of course entirely critical to the success of the project, but it was an area in which very little formal guidance was available. The principal method of knowledge acquisition was analysis of tape-recorded interviews of one of a number of experts solving a chosen batch of cases, and being asked to account for such features of their problem-solving as the similarities and differences between the decisions reached for the cases in that batch. The analysis resulted in a flowchart-like representation of that fragment of diagnosis, which the expert reviewed and modified if necessary.

The overall framework for the rulebase—the broad classes of fault and symptom—was acquired from one expert, a debug engineer chosen for his overall knowledge of the product and the test process. With the framework in place, he and a number of other experts, including some who had worked on the original design of the product, were used to 'fine tune' the rulebase.

Selection and filling-in of each portion of the knowledge base was done as follows: important classes of faults would be chosen by finding the five most common failure codes recorded over the preceding month in the failure analysis database. (This database existed before RBEST, the 'type of failure' code being entered by the debug technician; the quality of the diagnoses so entered has improved since RBEST.) 10 or more examples of these problems would be requested: each such example consisted of test reports and detailed reports of the actual repair, tests carried out, and so on. These would be analysed over the course of a few days to formulate detailed questions for the formal taped interviews: the test cases were typically only a starting point, with a large number of hypothetical questions also being asked ('What would you have said if these errors had occurred on another platter as well?'), and so they were far from being strict on-the-job protocols.

Each hour of recorded material usually required about 10 hours of analysis. The resulting flowchart-like representation was reviewed by the experts, modified (in that form) if necessary, and then coded as rules plus associated procedural data abstraction code. Once the information from an interview session had been incorporated into the system, it was then applied again to a growing battery of test cases, and discrepancies between the system's diagnoses and those of the expert could be used as the basis for the following interview session.

The detailed and explorative treatment of concrete cases proved to be a productive method of acquiring experts' problem-solving knowledge: they seemed to find it quite natural, and were able to answer most of the probing questions without difficulty. They seemed to relish the opportunity to demonstrate the depth and breadth of their knowledge— indeed, controlling the flow of detailed knowledge and amusing anecdote was a problem which made the taped record particularly valuable—but without frequent feedback from the improving system in which they could see their knowledge being incorporated, the experts could easily have lost interest in the exercise.

REPRESENTATION AND REASONING

RBEST's internal representation is straightforwardly shallow: the rulebase records direct associations between features of the input data and the likely cause of that collection of features; the textual output follows quite directly from the determination of likely cause, with only systematic variation—for example, the identification of a particular subassembly within a group of identical subassemblies. The determination of the value of each individual feature is entirely deterministic.

Although it was not used during the development of the system, Clancey's model of heuristic classification (Clancey 1985) provides a good framework in which to view the functioning of the system. This model proposes that the process of heuristic classification as applied to simple diagnosis consists of three stages: data abstraction, transforming low-level data into more abstract aggregates; a heuristic 'leap' from these aggregates to one of a number of relatively broad solution abstractions; and then a refinement of the chosen solution abstraction to a solution more precisely relevant to the particular situation. Clancey illustrates this process with the following diagram:

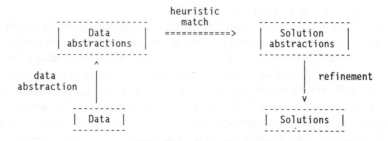

The organization of RBEST fits this model directly. The bulk of the data abstraction is performed deterministically in the 'data parsing' routines. A small number of higher-level data abstractions are also defined by the rulebase as simple boolean combinations of intermediate-level data abstractions. Combinations of these abstractions then appear directly in the conditional part of the main portion of the rulebase, which implements the heuristic match process, associating a given combination with a relatively detailed solution in a very few rule firings. Some degree of refinement of these solutions is produced by the instantiation of parameters; however, these differences in the solution are not reasoned about by the system itself, but produce variations in the textual output, which is interpreted by the users.

A considerable part of the solution refinement needed to fix the failure is implemented by the debug technician, under the guidance of fixed textual output produced by RBEST: thus, the conclusions of the RBEST rules are in many cases solution abstractions rather than full solutions. However, the RBEST system does not have access to the additional data required to specify a more exact solution, as the data are simply not present in the output of the routine test, but can only be obtained by performing further, more specialized tests: this is in line with the discussion of heuristic classification for diagnosis in Clancey (1985). Figure 7.3 illustrates this clearly: the repair process for the debug technician specifies additional tests to be performed, and nested conditional actions based on the result of these tests. Note that this entire text is output each time this rule fires, with the only modification being a small amount of instance-specific fault information at the position shown in the figure.

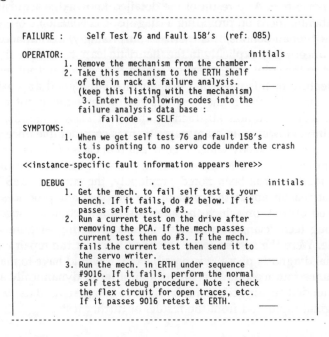

```
FAILURE :     Self Test 76 and Fault 158's  (ref: 085)

OPERATOR:                              initials
          1. Remove the mechanism from the chamber.  ___
          2. Take this mechanism to the ERTH shelf
             of the in rack at failure analysis.      ___
             (keep this listing with the mechanism)
          3. Enter the following codes into the
             failure analysis data base :
                failcode  = SELF
SYMPTOMS:
          1. When we get self test 76 and fault 158's
             it is pointing to no servo code under the crash
             stop.
<<instance-specific fault information appears here>>

   DEBUG  :          .                  initials
          1. Get the mech. to fail self test at your
             bench. If it fails, do #2 below. If it
             passes self test, do #3.                 ___
          2. Run a current test on the drive after
             removing the PCA. If the mech passes
             current test then do #3. If the mech.
             fails the current test then send it to
             the servo writer.                        ___
          3. Run the mech. in ERTH under sequence
             #9016. If it fails, perform the normal
             self test debug procedure. Note : check
             the flex circuit for open traces, etc.
             If it passes 9016 retest at ERTH.        ___
```

Figure 7.3 Output template showing complex conditional repair procedure

Inference control

The control of inference in RBEST is also easily explained within the heuristic classification model. All the raw data are available in the input file at no incremental cost, and the necessary abstractions are deterministic and inexpensive to compute: it is, therefore, possible to precompute them, rather than evaluate them on demand.

The heuristic matcher consists of about 130 rules. Their conditions are, by design, essentially mutually exclusive (as the knowledge acquisition process produces decision trees) and it has proved unnecessary to perform any conflict resolution among competing rules.

Uncertainty

The RBEST system makes no use of uncertainty in the inference process: the data abstraction process is entirely deterministic, and the raw input data is noise-free. As a result of the detailed knowledge acquisition and the deliberate focus on providing a diagnostic conclusion closely related to a set of repair actions, it is (perhaps surprisingly) also unnecessary to handle uncertainty explicitly in the 'heuristic leap' from data abstraction patterns to the solution abstraction which the printed output represents: it is a feature of this particular domain that (to a good approximation) it is possible for the human experts to interpret the input to RBEST and identify a solution abstraction, that is a class of faults, without uncertainty. However, in many cases there is considerable uncertainty in the domain as to exactly which member of that class of faults is present— that is, exactly what is the most efficient procedure to identify and fix the precise fault. As has been noted previously, the current RBEST system does not reason about this part of the process, but produces a sheet of printed output, on which the alternatives for action are specified for the debug technician, with some suggested ordering—Figure 7.3 is an example. Were the system to be extended to cover the repair as well as the initial diagnosis phase, it is possible that it would have to make some use of uncertain reasoning techniques in order to dynamically adjust its recommended repair actions in the light of 'suggestive' data, both from the original input and from the results of further tests.

Quantitative summary

The rulebase proper, which implements the heuristic match process, consists of about 130 rules, which distinguish between just under 100 different rectification procedures; most of the remaining rules are concerned with the higher-level data abstraction. As noted above, many of the individual rectification procedures are themselves complex conditional actions, but they are a single category as far as the RBEST representation is concerned. A small number of them are trivial—such as 'operator aborted test'. There are about 60 different data abstractions used in the rule conditions; five are numeric, eight are multivalued, and the remainder are two-valued. Not all are independent—for example, some of the two-valued ones are special cases of particular values of numeric or multivalued parameters of particular diagnostic significance. The number of data abstractions appearing in rule conditions varies from 1 to 12, with an average (mean) of just under 4. The distribution of the number of data abstractions appearing in the rules is roughly normal with 3, 4, and 5 conditions being most common, except that there is a large number (nearly 40) of rules which contain only a single condition.

USER INTERFACE

This has already been covered extensively; for ease of reference we summarize here that the system takes its input by file transfer from the test control computer, and produces a printed report which details an appropriate rectification procedure. This rectification procedure is divided into two sections: one for the test operators who administer the test, and another, not always present, for the debug technician who performs more complex test and repair if appropriate. Figures 7.2 and 7.3 are examples of the system's output.

EVALUATION

Against the initial objective of investigating the utility of expert systems technology, the project has certainly succeeded: the technology has provided the substantial productivity gains and cost savings detailed in the remainder of this section.

Evaluation against the more specific objectives of:

* less time spent on diagnosing and fixing each failing drive
* successful fix implemented more often by less skilled people
* fewer 'no fault found' units resubmitted for test with no satisfactory explanation of failure.

shows substantial gains since the introduction of RBEST, although it would not be accurate to attribute all the improvement over the last two years to the presence of RBEST alone. Certainly, substantially less time is now spent on diagnosis—RBEST's high-accuracy diagnosis is produced in under a minute, compared to typical times before its introduction of 20 minutes, with hours being not uncommon. More than 30% of all failures are corrected by test operators or production people responsible for particular sub-assemblies without any assistance from the debug technicians or debug engineers, and 90% of the remaining drives are fixed by the debug technicians without calling on the engineers. The 'No Fault Found' rate and the proportion of drives making multiple passes through the test–diagnose–repair–retest loop has fallen substantially. However, though it is clear that RBEST is a major contributor to these improvements, it is the continual quality improvement programme, of which RBEST is only a part, which is assessed by these measures.

As far as the system's own coverage and accuracy are concerned, in 1988 less than 0.2% of the thousands of drives analysed by RBEST failed to receive a report. Diagnostic accuracy over the year is over 97%, and indeed in the second half of the year there was only one week in which the percentage of accurate diagnoses dipped below 100% to 96%, giving an accuracy for that period of 99.8%. For the purpose of these figures, an 'accurate' diagnosis means that the sequence of operations detailed on the system's output was followed, and that this resolved the problem. As previously described, the sequence of operations recommended can be complex, and may be of the form 'try action 1; retest; if it still fails, try action 2; retest; if it still fails, try action 3'. A diagnosis is still considered accurate if the debug technician successfully tried action 3 immediately, knowing that in this case it was more likely to resolve the problem (and that it did not depend for its success on actions 1 or 2 having been performed!), although in these circumstances the debug technician may well raise an enhancement request against the RBEST system.

As far as financial returns are concerned, the figure of $1M mentioned in the abstract was derived from the volume of drives failed and the greatly reduced amount of technician labour relative to production volumes associated with the introduction of RBEST to the process. It does not include any allowance for the reduction of time spent by engineers in debug—let alone the benefits of allowing the engineers to concentrate on their primary job function in introducing process improvements; nor does it recognize the benefits of more timely and consistent tracking of production quality.

Finally, of equal importance to coverage, accuracy, and financial return is to consider what the system's users are saying. The test operators say that they could not live without it; RBEST is a very friendly interface to the system that greatly improves the operator's productivity. Similar statements are made by the technicians. Though some might not gloat about the system's apparent intelligence because they perceive it to be a threat to their job security, they all recognize that their productivity has improved significantly. The engineering community are the strongest advocates of the RBEST system. They know that any 'new' knowledge that they learn concerning the product or process can now be captured permanently in RBEST. They also appreciate the ability to plot trends in the process available in a matter of minutes from the data in RBEST's associated relational database which holds a full failure history—a task on which they used to spend hours, using less reliable manually entered failure codes. In assisting the operators and technicians in performing a more responsible and thorough job than previously, RBEST is directly enhancing their job satisfaction.

ORGANIZATIONAL ISSUES

System introduction and significance

The process of introducing innovation into an organization is rarely entirely smooth: it was certainly not free from organizational pressures in the case of RBEST. At the time the idea of an expert system to assist in the final test process was first mooted, AI technology was perceived by much of the local management as a research technology whose pay-off was far from well demonstrated but with a very high entry fee in terms of dedicated and non-standard hardware and software (if not ideology!). It was difficult to find examples of directly comparable systems which had been produced with relatively modest effort: the widely touted systems (R1/XCON, MYCIN, PROSPECTOR, and so on) were the results of much larger development efforts than that proposed for RBEST, whilst the widespread existence of successful systems produced with modest efforts was almost entirely anecdotal.

Nevertheless, the strong personal enthusiasm of the developer and the backing of his immediate manager acting as 'champion' secured approval for a modest experimental effort—up to three months of engineer's time—financed out of the 'give-it-a-fling' contingency portion of the R & D budget. The management champion was crucial in formulating the detailed project plan previously described, with its frequent demonstrable deliverables. These reduced the perceived risk, since the firm commitment at each stage extended only to the next milestone: within the time constraints of each stage, however, it left the developer free to experiment with various ways of achieving the next goal. This project structure fitted well with the evolutionary prototyping approach which is often used in the development of expert systems, and the early identification of the areas of uncertainty and their progressive resolution provided a degree of useful structure which is absent from the more extreme 'hack-it-and-see' approach. This kind of disciplined prototyping is well described and cogently argued for by Boehm (1988). The freedom of technical choice within agreed overall goals also fits well with HP's long-established style of Management By Objectives.

As the development project progressed and met its successive milestones, top management confidence increased; the speed and the diagnostic accuracy of the resulting final prototype were both well above their well-managed expectations, and the decision was taken to incorporate use of the final prototype into the production process for the low-volume product which it diagnosed. Since the two groups of users had been involved in the production of this and preceding prototypes, bringing it into use on this product was straightforward. The prototype continued to work well in production use.

The next hurdle was to secure commitment from both management and peers for the extension of the system to diagnose production failures on the high-volume product. This was not without its difficulties: one of the dangers of demonstrating good performance on the low-volume product proved to be fears from some people responsible for the manufacture and testing of the higher-volume product that differences between the two products meant it would not be possible to use the same approach as had succeeded on the low-volume product. One of the most visible elements of the investment required to extend the system to cope with the higher-volume product was the time required from experts, who were under considerable pressure to work directly on the introduction of the new product. Using the more detailed investment and return estimates from the initial development effort, it proved possible to persuade all those involved that the likely return from the investment in extending the system to cover the new product would be substantial, and secure their commitment: a decision which has been vindicated by the benefits now being experienced, as detailed above.

The RBEST system now plays an essential role in the manufacture of disk drives at DMD; without it, sustaining the current production rate would require considerable extra expenditure. In isolation, it is 'tactically' rather than 'strategically' important, in that its function could be performed in other ways, albeit at increased cost and with lower quality. However, the use of expert systems in manufacturing final test, not only to provide quality and productivity improvements in that function but as a way of providing consistent data on the impact on quality of manufacturing techniques and design improvements, is playing an increasingly important role in HP's manufacturing strategy, with a number of related developments now taking place within DMD and elsewhere within HP. Initial experience with RBEST and other systems is that transfer of a manufacturing process to another site is eased when a diagnostic system such as RBEST is transferred as part of the process.

Maintenance

The rulebase of the RBEST system is continually updated to maintain its coverage and accuracy. New failure modes and refinements to the repair process need to be incorporated: these come partly from changes in the manufacturing process, and partly from improved experience with the repair of a correctly identified fault. It is interesting to note that the latter class of enhancement has become necessary directly as a result of the system's success—it is providing a stable and more systematic framework for the classification of failures, and this makes it worthwhile for the debug engineers to use the system as a means of recording their evolving knowledge of efficient identification and repair strategies for particular classes of fault.

Updates to the rulebase are checked against a large (and growing) battery of test cases, which are recorded instances of previous failures. Regression testing of the updated rulebase against these test cases is more or less automatic, although some changes to the results are correct and desirable—for instance, when one single fault-class is broken down into a number of subclasses.

Maintenance is proving feasible, but can be time-consuming. This is partly because of the sheer number of detailed change requests concerning the recommended repair strategies; but it is also partly because some properties of the rulebase (for instance the non-overlapping nature of rule conditions) are manually maintained, and so changes to the rulebase may sometimes require considerable inspection and thought before being implemented. Various ways of improving the maintainability of the rulebase are under investigation: these include a possible reformulation of the knowledge-base to make the crucial rulebase properties structurally guaranteed rather than manually maintained, and the addition of a more sophisticated control strategy operating over a more structured description of the diagnosis space.

LESSONS LEARNT

Reasons for success

Factors in RBEST's favour included:

* the choice of a problem whose solution is of real economic value

* the use of controlled incremental prototyping
* strong support from immediate management
* the use of 'conservative' AI/ES technology: structured selection by simple pattern-matching, and no use of uncertainty—restrictions which were appropriate to the chosen problem!

Bottlenecks

Although the initial purpose of the project was to explore expert systems, becoming familiar with enough of the technology to implement a substantially useful system was not a major bottleneck. More difficult to overcome was the natural reluctance to introduce a new technology into a functioning manufacturing operation. Securing commitment for an initial investigation did not prove as great a stumbling block as the extension of the essentially proven prototype system from a 'backwater' product to the product whose production was critical to the division's success; it is most unlikely that this would have been possible without the detailed experience from the development of the prototypes.

Review of decisions and futures

The decisions taken throughout the development history of the project are ones which, even in retrospect, we believe are close to optimal in the circumstances under which they were taken. Of course, those circumstances include the degree of experience and support available at each point: were we embarking on another similar project now, with the experience of this and other projects behind us, there are some decisions which we would take differently, and many we would leave unaltered. (The question is not in fact hypothetical: we are currently investigating a number of systems similar to RBEST for other products being manufactured at the same site.)

Among the things we would leave unaltered is the use of controlled incremental prototyping as a development method. By 'controlled' we mean identifying from the outset the key technical and context-related uncertainties, and planning their stepwise resolution. The result of experience is rather to alter those things which we consider to be important uncertainties, and to give us more rapid and more reliable methods for resolving them. Thus, we would look more carefully at the intended use of the system and its role in the overall context, since— having established the usefulness of the technology—we are now in a position to look for problems whose resolution is important, and then filter these against a better (though still mainly intuitive) appreciation of the possibilities and limitations of the technology. We would again maintain close contact with the proposed users of the system, and would involve them even earlier in the process, since the purpose of the early 'technology proving' phases would be to establish the feasibility of the desirable rather than trying to make the feasible acceptable.

Experience with this and other diagnostic systems suggests the utility of a more explicit model of the 'reasoning' processes to be used by the system. These are often suggested by the approach of a particular expert, but they can also be a useful framework into which to fit a collection of isolated surface-level problem-solving behaviours. The framework of heuristic classification (Clancey 1985) on which is based the description of RBEST's representation and reasoning is one such model; even though it is at a rather high level of abstraction, it is useful in structuring the acquisition of diagnostic knowledge from an expert, in prompting the knowledge engineer to ask questions such as 'are there other failures like this one, and how do you tell them apart?', or 'what other patterns do you look for in this piece of data?'. We would also consider the use of more concrete and task-specific models of diagnostic problem-solving based on the hierarchical nature of the solution abstractions. We expect that the use of these models to structure the knowledge would improve both the knowledge acquisition process—in focussing the interviews and giving us a better feeling for what proportion of the domain we had tackled—and in the long-term maintenance of the system, in keeping the elements of the knowledge base structurally separated rather than needing to manually ensure their non-interference, as at present.

In addition to similar systems on different products, we are considering the utility and feasibility of extending the RBEST system to support the debug technician's repair process more extensively. This may involve no more than simple book-keeping on the repair alternatives which have proved most effective in resolving each failure category: it may also involve making that portion of the system interactively guide the debug technician through the repair process, rather than describing an entire, conditional repair process in textual form.

PERSONAL COMMENTS

Acknowledgements

We would like to thank Steve Germain who provided a very positive development environment and allowed Keith to learn the technology as he went along. We would also like to thank Mark Letcher, our primary expert, Dave Bradley, Andrew Spencer and Lee Roby for their expertise and their patience in sharing that expertise. There are several people who helped us get started by sharing their experiences in building expert systems: they include Marc Barman, Terry Cline, Roy VanDoorn, Joe Hinklin and George Tatge.

Special thanks must go to Dave Bohan who took a chance and changed his career path to learn LISP and expert systems: Dave and Keith make quite a team, and the whole RBEST effort would have been impossible without him.

CONCLUSIONS

The RBEST system is a successful application of modest rule-based programming techniques and direct expert-reviewed knowledge acquisition, which has been crucial in the expansion of production at HP's Disk Memory Division. In direct labour savings alone, it continues to produce a return on investment of six or seven times, and is expected to save at least another $1M in 1989: it has also played a considerable role in the continuing programme of quality improvement. Further systems are coming into operation at DMD based on the RBEST success, and are already playing a key role in making HP a leading long-term player in the supply of high-quality, low-cost disk drives.

REFERENCES

Boehm, B.W. (1988). 'A Spiral Model of Software Development and Enhancement'. *IEEE Computer*, May, 61–72.

Clancey, W.J. (1985). 'Heuristic Classification'. *Artificial Intelligence*, 27, 289–350.

Feigenbaum, E.A. and McCorduck, P. (1984). *The Fifth Generation*, Michael Joseph, London.

8

KANT: An Expert System for Telediagnosis

Jessica Ronchi, Graziella Butera
and Diego Lo Giudice

ABSTRACT

KANT is a distributed blackboard-based architecture designed to diagnose the communication board of an Olivetti L2 machine connected as a remote terminal to a host computer. KANT is a collection of knowledge-based systems: some of these operate in the field and are directly connected to the L2 machine, and the others operate back at the office and interact with the human experts. These diagnostic systems are configured in two blackboard systems which exchange data via the SNA link. Such architecture allowed us to solve the hard and expensive problem of diagnosing SW and HW malfunctionalities of communication boards in sites far from where the experts reside. In other words experts from the headquarters of Olivetti in this way are available to all subsidiaries and Olivetti customers around the world.

INTRODUCTION

The authors of this paper are members of the Olivetti Artificial Intelligence Center. The Center is physically split into two sites: Ivrea (Italy), where the basic goals are to develop Applications and Research studies with Italian Universities and Cupertino (California) which is more oriented to AI Products development as well as Research and development of joint projects with qualified research institutions.

Jessica Ronchi is currently a research staff member of the Natural Language group. She has been responsible for the KANT project development of which she was project leader. Previously, she designed and developed LAVOISIER an expert system for quality assurance. She received her MS in Computer Science from the University of Pisa.

Graziella Butera is currently responsible for applications of expert systems. She is project leader of PARMENIDE, an expert system for credit assessment developed for a large Olivetti banking customer. She has also contributed to the design of KAFKA, an expert system for board trouble-shooting. She received her MS in Computer Science from the University of Pisa.

Diego Lo Giudice is currently a research staff member of the Expert System Shells group. He is working on the design and development of CLEOPATRA, a powerful and user-friendly logic oriented tool for building knowledge based systems. He also contributed to the development of LEONARDO, an expert system for SW configuration. He also received his MS in Computer Science from the University of Pisa.

The KANT project started in November 1986, the prototype was ready by Summer, 1987 and was exhibited at IJCAI in Milan (Italy). It ended in January 1988. It has been developed at Ivrea in the Olivetti Systems and Network Division with cooperation between the AI group and the Communication group.

OBJECTIVES

The nature of the problem

The Olivetti L2 mini-computer (LSX) can be used as a remote terminal in a SNA network. Software communication is provided on the L2 machine on an intelligent board called LPU (Line Process Unit) in order to relieve the central unit from communication activities. The goal of KANT is to diagnose this communication subsystem satisfying all constraints imposed by the domain configuration.

Whenever a connected terminal does not behave properly, the customer requires assistance from the nearest Olivetti subsidiary. The technical staff at the remote site are not always able to understand the nature of the problem since this could be deeply hidden in the system's kernel. It is often necessary to talk over the phone with the project team at the company's headquarters, and sometimes a member of the project team must fly to the remote site to analyse the problem. This means higher costs for the subsidiary and lower productivity for the project team.

It is not easy trying to point out the appropriate specialists that can help to solve the problem. The origin of the fault could involve different parts such as the communication subsystem, the machine configuration, the hardware etc. each one requiring particular knowledge and then a particular specialist. The group in charge of the top-level layers of the communication subsystem after figuring out the trouble, involve the appropriate teams of specialists. This happens after the telephone call from the remote site reaches the group.

An important thing to note is that at any time, depending on the hypothesis that is currently held to be true, a number of different specialists are working together to fix the problem. The team of specialists involved is likely to change dynamically as the hypotheses are modified during the investigation.

The measure of success

At this point it is obvious that to understand how the whole process of detecting the fault and diagnosing it implies many manpower hours, meaning effective costs and degradation of productivity.

The Expert System development and application to the problem drastically reduces both. On one hand costs are reduced since specialists do not have to fly to where the problem happened. On the other hand telephone costs are drastically reduced. In fact, all telephone calls between the technician of the subsidiary and the people at the headquarters are avoided. Those calls were frequent, very expensive, and often useless because of misunderstandings between them (the technicians do not have enough knowledge to explain clearly what happened and to answer properly the specialists' questions). As will be described later, KANT queries directly the malfunctioning machine and acquires directly all data and information needed for solving the problem. At this phase the technician is involved by KANT with very easy questions about external and visible behaviours of the machine.

Productivity is increased since the specialists are not always involved when the fault occurs; 85% of cases are solved from KANT itself. Only for the remaining 15% do specialists have to be available and interact only and exclusively with KANT.

SYSTEM SPECIFICATION

From the strategic point of view the main goals of the KANT project are:

* to relieve the project team of most of the burden of troubleshooting (and so improve their productivity)

* to have a limited knowledge of the terminal at the subsidiary (in order to save training costs at thousands of Olivetti subsidiaries in the world).

Given the various constraints, KANT was conceived as a distributed system, meant to interact with two different users.

Briefly, the basic components of the system are a Remote Diagnostic System (R_KANT), residing on the debugging machine, which basically checks the state of the terminal and a Local Diagnostic System (L_KANT), which runs on a minicomputer at the company's headquarters. The technician of the subsidiary interacts with R_KANT and the project team interacts with L_KANT.

Roughly 60% of cases are solved at the remote site investigating the terminal state and interacting with the technician. All other cases are reported to L_KANT: some cases are solved by L_KANT itself; others require interaction with the experts. L_KANT in the most difficult cases behaves as a support tool for the SNA experts, considerably simplifying their task. Rather than simply providing them with a link to the debugger machine, L_KANT reasons about the remote system's report when the latter is not able to solve the problem by itself. Sometimes L_KANT asks R_KANT for more information. The local system is driven by a profound knowledge of the communication subsystem, whereas the remote system's knowledge is totally heuristic.

In contrast to the development of a traditional SW project, in developing an expert system we believe that producing initially a huge pile of specifications is meaningless. The specifications come out during the prototype development, and only when the prototype is complete are the specifications outlined and almost clear. Basically as a development methodology we chose to implement a prototype.

The global project was subdivided into three main phases:

1. phase 1, to identify the problem.
2. phase 2, to develop the prototype.
3. phase 3, to develop the final expert system, basically acquire all the remaining knowledge of the domain.

During phase 1 the global domain target was analysed in order to identify a meaningful subset for the prototype implementation. This analysis was carried out by three AI experts interacting for a few weeks with the 'domain experts'. During the next phases one of these AI experts was then involved for 100% of her time while the other two played the role of consultants.

The result of phase 1 was the design of a summary architecture for the expert system. The whole architecture happened to be the one of R_KANT, because we thought that having a system like R_KANT was already a good step.

The success of R_KANT convinced and encouraged us to do better, so we performed a closer and complete study of all the classes of problems in our telediagnosis communication malfunctionalities. The final result was the distributed dual-blackboard architecture consisting of a group of local knowledge-based systems (R_KANT) with the same architecture.

USE OF RESOURCES

In choosing the hardware and software solutions we had to consider not only the characteristics of the problem in hand, but also some constraints forced upon us by the environment in which the expert systems were to function.

The Olivetti subsidiary staff is equipped with a portable Olivetti computer with 640 Kbytes of memory, the so called 'debugger machine'. On the one hand, 640 Kbytes are not enough to fit a complex diagnostic system into, but on the other hand, the company would not change thousands of portable computers all over the world to accommodate a new piece of test software. So we decided to run part (R_KANT) of the expert system on the debugger machine and part (L_KANT) on an Olivetti LSX mini-computer.

The prototype was developed in a Prolog which allowed the linking of 'C' procedures (Oli-Prolog). This was forced on us by the need for:

* speed of execution
* ability to call procedural code from within the rules.

Both parts of the expert system (R_KANT and L_KANT) make use of procedural code. L_KANT must verify the state of all communication protocol levels at fault time and therefore must analyse the SNA trace and the datascope trace. R_KANT interacts directly with the fault machine and so directly checks its memory and state.

The development team was organized as follows:

* a knowledge engineer (AI specialist), as project leader
* two groups of two persons, in each group a knowledge engineer and an apprentice.

The project leader structured the project so that the two groups could work independently: within the target domain a number of subdomains were identified and each assigned to one or other group.

Each group had to acquire the knowledge, implement, test and debug the knowledge base and then document the implemented system. The project leader not only identified and divided the subdomains between the two groups, but was also responsible for the integration of the finalized parts. The design methodology used was to develop a prototype on a subdomain of the target domain.

The criteria used in the selection of the subdomains were essentially two:

* highlight the significant and characteristic aspects of the target domain
* exclude aspects dependent on special situations.

The policy upheld in the development of the prototype was to not distinguish development and delivery environments, but to develop directly in the delivery environment.

INVOLVEMENT OF USERS

As mentioned previously, the methodology used in the development of KANT was to identify a subset of the target domain and to develop a prototype. The development of the prototype ended with a testing phase of the same prototype.

During this testing phase the future users of the expert system played a dominant role. More precisely, we identified a 'pilot user base' whose feedback proved useful for both the tuning of the knowledge base and the features to provide for the users.

As the conclusion of the development of the prototype we posed the following queries:

* coverage and accuracy of the knowledge base

* impact on the user of the expert system.

The success of the expert system lay in a satisfactory answer to the two queries.

In the absence of a pre-defined model we oriented ourselves towards an empirical model, and as such we selected a sample set of pilot users.

The group was composed of both 'domain experts' and 'domain non-experts'. The composition of the group was so decided for two reasons:

* KANT was directed at these two types of user

* we were interested in the two levels of feedback:

  (a) with respect to the 'domain experts' we wished to verify the coverage and accuracy of the knowledge base

  (b) whereas with respect to the 'domain non-expert' we wished to verify the exhaustiveness of the explanations presented by the expert system and the user friendliness.

The 'domain experts' were chosen from those who had collaborated during the development of the prototype. Meanwhile the only prerequisite for the 'domain non-expert' was that they were willing to rely on the AI technology in order to obtain constructive suggestions.

We installed four 'pilot stations' which were used for the day-to-day work activity of the pilot users.

At the conclusion of each day's work the corrections and suggestions were collected. With regard to the knowledge base we most often found ourselves faced with problems of coverage rather than problems of accuracy.

The 'domain non-expert' suggestions were useful on two fronts:

* the definition of an easily accepted user interface

* the treatment of certain situations which we had glossed over, believing them to be trivial.

KNOWLEDGE ACQUISITION

Knowledge sources for the project were multiple:

a) Kernel designers
b) Configuration and application experts
c) HW experts
d) Communication subsystem designers
e) SNA protocol experts
f) Technical documents.

Each of these areas was treated in different ways because the nature of the knowledge was different, experts of some areas were more available than others, some areas had granular knowledge spread among several experts, and finally some knowledge was documented. Basically our approach with human experts was to interview them and sometimes to study and observe their behaviour during their work.

Let us briefly cover all cases:

Knowledge acquisition in case (a) was easy enough. The expert was unique, available and very precise. He felt involved and was positively influenced by the new AI technology. The expert system covering this area was the most complex one, and included a lot of heuristic knowledge.

Knowledge acquisition in cases (b) and (c) was also straightforward but for different reasons. There were several experts, but the domain knowledge was simple and easy to understand. Experts in these areas were not frequently available because of other important tasks.

In cases (d) and (e) we had a difficult time. There were several experts and they were not very convinced about our AI approach. Their fear was of losing their job. Our impression is that they did not themselves perceive the need for a knowledge-based approach but they were forced to do so by their manager. Moreover, they were very busy and often not available. Often they gave us books and technical documents to read instead of explaining and helping us in understanding and modelling the knowledge.

In general when conflicts occurred among multiple experts, we explicitly treated the conflicts by putting the experts in front of each other until they arrived at a solution. In this case, often more than one solution did emerge (reflecting the various opinions), and we had to investigate further in order to assign a numerical priority factor to each solution.

ARCHITECTURE

The architecture and the control strategy of the system reflects the reality of the domain. The knowledge as previously seen can be semantically split in several areas and led us to decide to develop our expert system for each area. As a consequence since the areas were related to each other in some way, an optimal cooperation strategy among them was needed. We found the most efficient and suitable approach, as we will see, to be a blackboard architecture.

Behaviour and reasoning

As we have already said both L_KANT and R_KANT are a collection of cooperating rule-based systems, i.e. systems that deal with a specific aspect of the diagnosis and exchange their interpretation of the data until a complete solution is obtained. The two systems are based on a similar, blackboard-oriented, architecture.

The blackboard supports a shared database through which the various knowledge sources (in our case, the various rule-based systems) exchange information. The blackboard contains a list of the partial goals which are currently being pursued and the partial results so far obtained. In R-KANT, according to the partial results so far available, the scheduler (which is itself a rule-based system) selects one of the other rule-based systems and sets the new partial goal. In L-KANT the knowledge sources will instead turn on when the stored information matches their preconditions. In both cases any new partial results are recorded on the blackboard, and the process is repeated.

The remote system

R-KANT is composed basically of five rule-based systems, four of them are called 'specialists' and one is the scheduler:

1. The Scheduler has knowledge about the specialists' knowledge. At any time it can decide which specialist is more likely to solve the problem, given the current knowledge of the problem and given the domain knowledge of each specialist. R-KANT's scheduler is rule-based: its knowledge base contains information about the problems or subproblems that each remote specialist is capable of solving, and the new information that each of them is capable of providing. Its rules also specify which decisions must be taken when new information is

added to the blackboard. In particular, rule-based forward reasoning leads to a decision as to which specialist must be activated, or if it is necessary to pass control to the local system.

2. The Kernel Specialist which covers errors due to the kernel of the operating system on the LPU board. This rule-based system checks for memory contents, in particular registers, automata descriptors, event descriptors and the stack. It reads these directly from the memory of the faulted machine through a debug system. Then it determines the automaton that was active at crash time, its logic name and its state. In some cases it also analyses the system stack in order to rebuild the sequence of procedure calls before the fault occurred, and to identify the last procedure that was called. This specialist reasons forward from the data to perform further debug operations that provide more data, until, eventually, this process leads to a conclusion. All information is left on the blackboard as facts.

3. The Reply Code specialist interprets the codes received from the operating system that can be caused by an incorrect application program.

4. The Configuration specialist diagnoses inconsistencies in the software and hardware configurations and it also provides the actual values of all interesting configuration parameters. It is the only one that can consult the internal configuration file.

5. The Hardware specialist diagnoses hardware faults of the terminal.

In distinction to the Kernel Specialist the last three specialists have the same internal architecture. They are all backward-chaining systems. Each of these rule-based systems basically relies on heuristic knowledge.

The local system

L-KANT is a collection of six rule-based systems based on deep knowledge of the communication subsystem: three of them (Trace systems) analyse the trace produced at the SPH_SNA, SNA and SDLC layers, the other three (Code Systems) are experts on the software that implements the protocols. In particular they are:

1. The Trace Systems:
   The SPH_SNA, SNA and SDLC rule-based systems analyze the external trace in order to understand what happened before and during fault time. The external trace is provided by a datascope

connected to the physical communication line between the remote terminal and the host. The Trace systems, on the basis of this information attempt to identify the state of all communication protocol levels at fault time, in terms of the FSA (finite state automata) that describe them. Once they have determined the state they may be able to determine where the problem is (in the host application, in the protocol's code or if a configuration mismatch has occurred).

2. The Code Systems:
   These three rule-based systems deal with pieces of code relative to three layers of the communication subsystem. These rule-based systems know the communication subsystem's structure in terms of functions that handle each single protocol state, and the relations between them. They read from the blackboard the information they need (the machine state, the protocol state, the application request, current available hypotheses on the fault's cause) and try to identify the piece of code that is responsible for the fault.

Knowledge representation and implementation

KANT is implemented in Oli-Prolog (a 'C' version of Prolog). Oli-Prolog is an extension of the standard C-Prolog because it includes a superset of the standard built-in predicates.

All knowledge in KANT is represented by production rules, having the following syntax:

    IF <ANTECEDENT>
    THEN <CONSEQUENT>
    PRIORITY <number>
    COMMENT <string>

The ANTECEDENT of each rule includes the possibility of using both conjunctive and disjunctive predicates, while the CONSEQUENT allows only conjunctive predicates.

The PRIORITY values are used by the inference engines for conflict resolution (pick the rule with higher priority). No uncertainty reasoning is performed, numerical values are provided for choosing the best rules at every moment. The COMMENT is used during explanations.

Facts are represented by:

```
FACT<CONJUNCTIVE PREDICATES>
COMMENT<string>
```

As can be seen the formalism we adopted does not respect the Prolog syntax, in fact we developed a meta-interpreter in Prolog in order to allow such formalism. The purpose of that is to have more clear, explicit, explainable and maintainable knowledge bases.

The meta-interpreter performs also forward chaining on the rules.

The number of rules and facts is approximately 800.

The interface

The interface of KANT is basically menu-driven. In order to achieve a more friendly and highly interactive user interface, KANT uses the built-in windowing predicates offered by our Oli-Prolog.

At every moment the user can ask for the following information:

* the blackboard contents; that is all the knowledge inferred at that point of the execution and the goals that are going to be achieved
* explanations about the decisions taken by the specialists and by the scheduler system
* why the system is asking the current question
* the rules that the system applied in order to achieve the current goal.

When one of the above requests is made, a dedicated window appears.

When KANT queries the user for some data, the user can choose between two alternatives. He can select the answer among one of the hints supplied by the system in a menu, or he can type it from the keyboard (the latter way is used when the menu does not contain the appropriate answer).

EVALUATION AND LESSONS LEARNT

Solving a problem of telediagnosis without KANT meant spending days and sometimes weeks: identification of the human specialists, repetitive telephone calls, travel of the specialists in some cases, and finally time needed to solve the problem. Most of these steps are avoided with KANT, and in the worst cases experts can have on-line feedback on their terminal through KANT with all the hints and support provided by it. KANT itself now identifies the teams or experts that have to be involved in order to solve the problem, cutting out a number of people from the whole process. This results in a great deal of time saved using KANT which for diagnosing a remote terminal in an average problem can even take less than a few hours.

In order to give a more appropriate evaluation, let us consider three basic classes of errors (based on the time they need to be solved).

1. Errors that can be solved by R_KANT itself

2. Errors that can be solved by L_KANT and R_KANT, where R_KANT acts as a server for L_KANT

3. Errors that can be solved by KANT with the intervention of the experts of Communication (that means L_KANT, R_KANT and experts all involved together).

Errors of the first class needed previously a couple or more days to be solved (most of the time was lost in individualizing the problem through telephone calls). With Kant in the same case it takes less than 30 minutes. Errors of the second class previously needed from two to four weeks (often experts from the headquarters had to fly down, and most of the time was spent in interpreting the trace of the communication line). KANT now does this by itself; the time needed to solve the same problem is just the execution time needed for receiving through the communication line the information from R_KANT, interpreting the trace and solving the problem. The whole process is done in a few hours.

Finally the third class of errors are special cases and a precise average cannot be given. Previously the time needed could even be months. With KANT we reduce drastically the analysing phase and the individualizing of the experts. The time needed to solve the problem completely depends on the experts. In any case, above all, experts have much more reliable information available with KANT.

As mentioned previously, a first important evaluation was done when we first conceived the system as a unique one in the remote site. The evaluation of this prototype was so successful that we decided to enlarge and treat a greater class of problems also covering faults that were diagnosed locally at the headquarters in Ivrea.

The success was justified since more than 55 to 60% of cases were solved by the first KANT running only in the remote sites. These results convinced us and the top management that some experts of Ivrea could save even more time if we were able to advise them or relieve them of some tedious and repetitive work. Initially the experts involved in the development of L-KANT were basically hostile to the new AI approach. More precisely, AI was an unknown technology to some of them and they just refused completely to cooperate; others who had a surface knowledge of expert systems were afraid to lose their important role of experts of communication in telediagnosis. In other words, they were not available to reveal to us the secrets and heuristics that they had developed over years of experience.

Finally the whole project was forced upon them by the top management, they were not prepared for the new approach and above all they were not relieved from their daily routine work in order to cooperate with us.

These are the basic reasons why the development of L_KANT was hard and slow. It took a lot of patient hours of interviewing and study in order to gather the necessary knowledge for the development of L_KANT. The refinement phase has been the most important for the development of L_KANT. Only when the experts could use the first prototype did they understand the importance and the role of the expert system and give us a substantial feedback. Such feedback allowed us to improve KANT.

A final evaluation was done at the end of the system (results were also evaluated during the whole development of the project). The evaluation showed us that the 15% of problems not totally covered by KANT happened to fall in the field of the Communication subsystem designers and SNA protocol experts (code expert systems). The result was expected since this was a difficult area to treat in the knowledge acquisition phase. It turns out that some problems of this 15% are too complex to be solved by the expert system technology.

The system's architecture turns out to be well suited and completely adequate for the problem. A new idea is being studied in order to improve and generalize the use of KANT.

The communication group is studying a formal specification language for the existing communication protocols and for new ones. If this is successfully done, we will provide KANT with knowledge of the specification language, so KANT will be able to work on all kinds of communication protocols defined with the specification language. This will allow us also to represent better and more precisely the code knowledge of the communication protocols.

No further development on KANT is in progress, since we are waiting for the specifications to be developed and then the protocol code to be rewritten.

Our experience has shown us how the role of experts is extremely important in the development of an expert system. We believe that the first people who have to be convinced and become enthusiastic about a new methodology must be the experts. Experts have to be motivated and ready to be protagonists during the development of an expert system. Another important factor of course is the participation and the conviction of the top management, which has to be ready to invest money and resources.

ORGANIZATIONAL ISSUES AND CONCLUSIONS

The project was developed jointly by the AI group and the Communication group both in the Olivetti Systems and Network division.

The AI team gave the AI know-how while the Communication group offered the domain experts. The idea of applying the expert systems technology to the communication problems originated in the Communication management. The AI specialists studied and confirmed the applicability of the AI technology to the problem and offered its resources and support.

As already mentioned alternatives to the AI approach were much more expensive (e.g. training all subsidiary staff in the world).

The expert system described in this chapter turned out to be successful. The advantages proposed by the expert system technology all seem to be verified.

The whole system is maintainable, some experts of the communication group have acquired the necessary AI know-how in order to maintain the knowledge bases themselves. Supervision of the AI specialist is, however, still necessary.

The system was also being used by the experts to train new people joining the communication group. This is possible using the explanations provided by KANT, which are clear and detailed.

The architecture of KANT has proved very interesting to the AI community, and can be considered as a valid suggestion in other communication problems in networking or similar diagnosis tasks.

BIBLIOGRAPHY

Davis, R. Diagnostic Reasoning based on structure and behaviour. *Artificial Intelligence*, 24.

Hayes-Roth, B. *BB1: An Architecture for Blackboard Systems*, Stanford Report STAN-CS-84-1034.

Hayes-Roth, B. Blackboard Architecture for control. *Artificial Intelligence*, 26.

Nii, H.P. (1986). *Blackboard Systems*. Stanford Report KSL-86-18.

Reiter, R. A Theory of Diagnosis from First Principles. *Artificial Intelligence*, 32, No.1.

De Kleer, J. Diagnosing Multiple Faults. *Artificial Intelligence*, 32, No.1.

9

Aries Club Case History

Gary Chamberlin and Richard Lelliott

ABSTRACT

Aries was the Alvey IKBS community club set up to explore the usefulness of expert systems in the insurance industry. During the period 1985 to 1987, the Club successfully developed two new prototype systems—the applications being, respectively, fire insurance underwriting and the selection of equities for an investment portfolio. The work of the Club during this period is summarized, including the two systems, their design, implementation and commercial relevance. Such aspects as knowledge acquisition and representation, development and delivery environments, system evaluation and the organizational issues are discussed. The main lessons and conclusions from the 1985–87 experience are drawn out, in particular its usefulness as a vehicle for awareness and learning.

INTRODUCTION

Who we are

The Aries Club was one of the Community Clubs first set up under the Alvey IKBS Programme. The purpose of these Clubs was to promote awareness of expert systems in various industrial sectors—for Aries, the industry served was insurance (Aries = Alvey Research for Insurance Expert Systems). The club is unusual in that it survived the ending of Alvey and is still in active existence today.

Gary Chamberlin is a Research Fellow at the City University. He served as the Secretary of Aries and is now its Project Manager. Richard Lelliott is a manager in the computer department of the Sun Alliance Insurance Group. He was formerly a Principal Consultant with Logica Financial Systems, and was the Project Manager for the Aries work described in this chapter.

Where and when the project was done

The main project work was carried out at the offices of Logica in London. In addition, there were many visits to the participating insurance companies to carry out the expert interviews. Other locations such as City University and the Institute of Actuaries were used for conferences, Club meetings, and workshops.

The project proper began in September 1985 and ended in June 1987. However, there was a significant start-up effort, and initial studies for the project were done in the period March to May 1985.

OBJECTIVES

What we were trying to do

The primary goal of the project was to promote awareness of expert systems technology within the UK Insurance Industry. The mechanism for achieving this goal was the building of two expert systems, one each in the fields of life and general insurance. The systems, however, were intended as *prototypes*, and not as fully operational systems ready for immediate use in the office.

Complementary aims were to test and prove the value of expert systems to insurers, and to prove that such systems can be delivered cost effectively.

The nature of the problem to be solved

The general insurance application was the underwriting of commercial fire risks. The main aim of the expert system was to make head office underwriting skill and expertise available at the branch level.

The life insurance application was on the investment side, and tackled the selection of equities for the office's portfolio. The aim of the system was to provide an expert assistant for the fund manager or senior analyst. It should enable him to be more consistent in his work, and to review more companies' shares in a given time.

How success was to be measured

Both experts and users should be satisfied with the systems and their manner of operation.

Companies should be happy with the progress and development of the project as a whole. (A survey carried out at the end of the project showed that approximately 90% of the companies involved were satisfied in this way.) At the end of the project, companies should take up the systems (a) for use as demonstrators, and (b) as bases for further development.

The Club should achieve a high profile for its activities and the results of its work. There should be follow-on projects put into effect by a later extension of the Club's activities.

SYSTEMS SPECIFICATION

Scope of the problem and context within the organization

Fire risks system

The system was being built at a time of change for the fire insurance industry. The main feature was the demise in July 1985 of the Fire Offices' Committee (effectively a cartel) and its Tariff of recommended premium rates.

In its most general terms, the problem was that the head office underwriters were overloaded, and wanted to delegate expertise to branch level. For many of the risks proposed, simple rate-book underwriting could not be sufficient, and better support tools were needed at branch level. Consistency of working between different underwriters and branches was a further goal to be served by the system.

For the purposes of Aries, a decision was taken to limit the system to risks in one industry only, the clothing industry. This was felt to be a sufficiently difficult but self-contained part of the overall problem on which to work. The results should be easily extendable to deal with fire risks in other industries.

The output of the system should be either rejection of the risk proposed, or its acceptance at a suggested rate. This rate could be expressed as being equal to a standard base rate, or as the standard rate modified by a premium or a discount, as appropriate.

Equity selection system

The background to the building of the system was the de-regulation of the Stock Exchange (October 1986), and the increased scale of international competition in the investment field. The fund manager's problem was that of being able to move rapidly enough in a fast-moving global market. His work involved much repetitive analysis of base data on companies and company shares, which might reasonably be automated by an expert system.

Consistency of working was again a desirable goal.

A decision was taken to limit the Aries system to dealing with manufacturing and distribution companies in the UK. The system should tackle the first two of three analytical operations:

a) Analysis of Extel data

b) In-depth (prospective) analysis

c) Confirmation check with colleagues, and against the insurance company's own investment strategy.

Results from the system should be expressed as Buy/No Buy advice on various portfolios within the overall fund operation. Decisions (and underlying reasoning) should relate to clear criteria, namely:

Buy for growth/ Buy for income/ Buy for recovery/Buy for discount in share price to actual assets
(If no criteria are satisfied, result is No Buy)

Degree of confidence in decision should be expressed in the form of a price limit, e.g. Buy provided price is less than X (a stated figure).

Who produced the specification

Fire risks system

The specification was produced by the experts working with the development team.

Equity selection system

The specification was produced by the experts working with the development team, but was also discussed and modified by the Club's Steering Committee.

How it altered as the project progressed

Fire risks system

Changes were in the nature of refinement rather than alteration. There was a deepening of the knowledge base as the work continued.

Equity selection system

Following the initial studies, there was a change of expert at Day 1 of the project proper. This led to a new, and completely different approach to equity selection.

As work progressed, it proved necessary to limit the depth, in order to preserve confidentiality of the most detailed expertise. Concentration on broad structure was also necessary, so that elicitation and testing could be done within the time available from the leading expert.

The Aries Technical Coordinators suggested technical improvements, e.g. the parameterization of the knowledge base, and these were mostly adopted.

The evaluation criteria at the start of the project

Fire risks system

It should be possible to formalize the underwriters' knowledge.

It should be possible to create a good working prototype.

Both experts and users should be satisfied with the system and its manner of operation.

At the end of the project, companies should take up the system (a) for use as a demonstrator, and (b) as a basis for further development.

Equity selection system

It should be possible to formalize the investment manager's knowledge.

It should be possible to create a good working prototype.

The experts (who are also the users in this case) should be satisfied with the system and its manner of operation.

At the end of the project, companies should take up the system (a) for use as a demonstrator, and (b) as a basis for further development.

USE OF RESOURCES

Hardware and software environment for system

The development environment for both systems was Kee on a Sperry/Unisys Explorer. Significant work in each system was also done by dropping out of Kee into the underlying Lisp language.

For delivery, the Kee/Explorer environment was unacceptable, and porting of both systems to the IBM-PC was carried out. For Fire Risks the shell Crystal was used, and for Equity Selection Leonardo was the chosen shell.

Selection of hardware and software

The development environment was chosen after an extensive evaluation exercise. This involved looking at the merits of shells versus high-level toolkits versus AI languages. The languages were rejected as being too risky for a limited time and cost project such as Aries, while the shells available at the time (December 1985) were rejected as not being sufficiently powerful. This left the high level toolkits, and the Kee/Explorer combination was chosen after further evaluation of the possibilities on a price/performance basis.

The delivery environments were chosen after a brief evaluation of PC-based shells available or in immediate prospect at the time (December 1986). The IBM-PC with PC-DOS was chosen as the only machine/operating system with sufficient commonality among the Aries Club members.

Integration with other software

Very little integration at all was possible using the Aries Kee version (#2) on the Explorer. Crystal and Leonardo both allowed links with data bases, spreadsheets etc, to be made. Implementing such links was, however, beyond the intended scope of the Aries project.

Staff recruitment and training

Staff were provided by Logica, which already had people of an appropriate level of skill and experience in its project teams. The skills were augmented by Kee training, and by recourse when necessary to Logica's Cambridge research department.

The design method used

Both projects made extensive use of paper models (intermediate knowledge representations) created by the knowledge engineers. The paper models were tested out by reference back to the experts, in an iterative procedure. Machine prototypes followed at a short remove in time (two to three weeks at most), and the iterations continued. The whole procedure can be described as a disciplined and iterative prototyping exercise, with emphasis on the importance of the paper model as an intermediate stage.

Staff organization

A business manager retained overall control of the Logica operation. Responsibility for the technical project work was devolved to a project manager. Under the latter, two separate but closely relating teams worked—one on knowledge elicitation and the other on system implementation.

Development as opposed to delivery environments

The actual environments used are described above. Kee/Explorer was found to be a powerful tool for development. It was, however, too slow in operation to be suitable for delivery. Besides this, Aries Club members were not willing to purchase this type of equipment, and the system integration facilities were very poor. Hence the necessity for a distinct delivery environment.

The delivery tools were able to reproduce the main functionality of the two systems on the PC. But the user interfaces lacked the high quality of Kee, and there were difficulties with such features as 'What-If?' and default setting in the Fire Risks port.

INVOLVEMENT OF USERS

The stages at which users were involved

In the Fire Risks system, users were involved from the start of the detailed elicitation and design phases. In Equity Selection, the experts themselves were the users, and were involved from the very beginning.

The role of users

The users' roles were seen as being very important. These were, first, to help mould and improve the user interface, and second to help test the system for usability, completeness and accuracy.

KNOWLEDGE ACQUISITION

How knowledge was acquired

The techniques used were structured interviewing, together with a modified form of protocol analysis. A sketch-plan for the course of each interview was made in advance, and each interview was followed by an extensive debriefing session. Two knowledge engineers were present throughout, which was found to aid the flow at the interviews. The interviews were recorded, in order to allow full checkback on the various points arising. The recordings were not transcribed, and were returned to the experts at the end of the project.

The use of examples and case studies throughout was found to be a vital element in the procedure. Analysis of the knowledge once elicited was done via paper modelling and prototyping, as described above under 'The design method used'.

Dealing with conflicts between multiple experts

In each case, the Aries expert teams consisted of one lead expert and two moderating experts. The experience of the two teams differed markedly, however—thus in the Fire Risks project, the experts agreed in large measure and resolved any minor conflicts by themselves.

In Equity Selection, the lead expert's view agreed reasonably well with that of one of the moderators. The other moderator had an entirely different approach to the problem. The only practical course was to adopt the lead expert's view throughout, since to have tried to combine it with that of the second moderator would have led to disaster. (A second equity selection system, quite different from the first and probably equally valid, could have been built using the second moderator's approach.)

Availability of expert knowledge

In Fire Risks, the expert knowledge was made fully available, within the allotted time constraints. In Equity Selection, there were areas of knowledge which the expert preferred not to probe too deeply, for confidentiality reasons. The time constraints were also a good deal tighter. This is not surprising, given the pace of work in the investment field today, and Aries counted itself lucky to find even one leading expert willing to give the necessary time and attention to the project.

Experts' reaction to knowledge elicitation process

Fire risks

The experts' initial nervousness soon turned to enthusiasm. They found that the knowledge elicitation helped them gain a better understanding of their own jobs. Also, they found increased confidence through discussion of underwriting problems with other experts.

Equity selection

An initial scepticism on the part of the experts was dispelled as the work proceeded. Their interest was held and increased by the appearance of machine prototypes. On the downside, however, the lead expert's nervousness over releasing confidential knowledge increased during the course of the project.

The experts were pleased with the resulting system, but showed a reluctance to test the model properly. This was mainly because of the considerable extra time that full testing requires.

REPRESENTATION AND REASONING

The high-level model of the problem constructed

More origami—the paper models again! Essentially, these models are conceptual diagrams, showing the path taken through the problem, and the relationship of the various determining factors. As the work develops, so the structure unfolds, and the rules which are relevant at the different junctures can be written down. Apart from diagrams and rules, other elements such as decision tables and cash flow formulae also form parts of the paper model.

The representation chosen

The machine representation consisted of rules and frames. The knowledge elicitation showed that both domains were rule-based, hence rules were appropriate. Frames were used in addition as giving a convenient structural framework for the problems.

The control structure used

Fire risks

Control was achieved by limited forward chaining within procedures. Backward chaining was also considered, but problems arose with Kee under the required interface. The problem was later solved, in time for the Equity Selection work. (By doing so, the Aries team broke new ground in the uses of Kee.)

Equity selection

Control is by free forward chaining on the first pass through the system, i.e. the Extel analysis. Also, active values (demons) are used within a procedural skeleton.

Uncertainty

Perhaps surprisingly, the Aries team found no uses for formal uncertainty methods within its two systems. The reasons appear to be as follows. We can divide the determining factors in both systems into the objective ones, and those containing subjective valuation. Examples of objective factors are building materials in Fire Risks, and accounting ratios in Equity Selection. For these, there is by definition no uncertainty, always provided that the information can be obtained.

On those factors with subjective valuation, an example in both systems is the quality of management. Here again, given an expert who is capable of making his valuation, there is no uncertainty to speak about. The uncertainty only enters when either there is (a) no information, or (b) no expert. The Aries systems are, quite deliberately, not constructed for use under such conditions. Almost as confirmation of the above, the Aries experts refuted attempts to introduce standard types of uncertainty into the systems.

Finally, the aim of both systems is to gauge the probability of an event within a limited time-frame. Hence, for a mathematical treatment, standard probability methods would seem to be more appropriate than one of the new uncertainty calculi.

Quantitative summary

The bare statement of the number of rules in an expert system is not necessarily a good guide to its size. With this caveat, the Aries statistics are as follows:

> Fire Risks: 128 Kee Rules + 515 other Kee units, porting to 349 Crystal Rules.
> Equity Selection: 190 Kee Rules + 734 other Kee units, porting to 450 Leonardo Objects.

USER INTERFACE

The sort of user model implemented

No explicit user modelling was done in the Aries project. In the Fire Risks system the user level assumed is that of junior branch underwriter. In Equity Selection, the questions can be answered at various levels, depending on the expertise of the user. The system has been essentially constructed on the assumption that the user will be a well qualified expert in his own right.

Explanation facilities provided

A 'Help' function is available throughout both systems, though it is not fully instantiated.

A 'How?' function is available to a high level of detail in both systems, but again is not fully instantiated.

A 'What If?' function is comprehensively implemented in the development systems, but not in the ported version of Fire Risks.

The use of natural language/graphics/mice/interactive video etc

The Aries systems do not use natural language or interactive video at all. The development systems are fully mouse-driven in a WIMP-type (Windows–Icons–Mouse–Pull-down menus) environment. The ported versions employ multiple choice windows driven from the keyboard.

EVALUATION

Performance as opposed to objectives

The Club's main target of bringing awareness of expert systems to the UK Insurance Industry was well achieved. There was general satisfaction with the systems produced as prototypes in the given application areas. The satisfaction was common amongst all concerned, whether experts, users or developers.

The chosen mechanism for porting the systems, i.e. via a paper model, was proved as both viable and effective.

Evaluation of value to the organization

An evaluation of the Fire Risks system showed that the system was generally seen to be valid by Club members. Different modes of organization in the different companies meant that the system was much better adapted to some than to others.

A survey carried out at the end of the project by consultants Arthur Young showed a very high level of member satisfaction in Club activity *per se*.

The stage at which evaluation was carried out

The Fire Risks evaluation was done in Summer 1986, following the main development of this system (but before the ported version was created). The Arthur Young survey was effected at the close of project (May to June 1987).

No formal evaluation of the Equity Selection system was carried out.

As result of evaluation what we would do differently

If the project was re-done with the same start and end dates, very little would be changed by us. If, however, the project were to start again now, it is likely we would use different hardware and software development tools, as so much more is now available.

We would not change the personnel or the management techniques.

Early in the project, the awareness workshops were beneficial for Club members, but tended to disrupt project work. A more careful balancing of priorities would, therefore, be needed in this respect. Later on in the project, the workshops worked well from all points of view.

The use of the system in practice

As already mentioned, there was no aim in the first place to produce immediately operational systems—experimental/demonstrator-type sytems only were intended.

The Arthur Young survey indicated, however, that two companies at least had developed the Fire Risks system and were using it in the office. The survey, however, was confidential, and full information on this subsequent development is not available.

The current state

Both systems have been delivered to all members, in the form of full listings of the Kee code. Regrettably, the systems are not executable in this form, since no Aries Club member is (or was at the time) in possession of an Explorer or the Kee environment itself. Also, paper models of both systems have been distributed, with exhaustive reports on the development exercise.

Ported versions of both systems have been delivered in run-time form for use on the IBM-PC. Development versions have also been provided for further experimentation by member companies. (Many possess copies of Crystal and/or Leonardo for this purpose.)

Future developments

A new Club for developing cooperating expert systems in investment was organized by Logica. The Club was called 'Taurus', and carried out a pilot investigation during 1987–88. However, this work has not proceeded any further.

An extension of the Aries Club itself was organized at City University, called 'Aries at City'. This initiative has continued the awareness work of the original Aries. It has developed new expert systems in Life Underwriting and Personal Financial Planning and is currently developing a Pensions Legislation Adviser.

ORGANIZATIONAL ISSUES

The politics of introducing innovation

An expert systems awareness programme is an important means for dispelling fear, uncertainty and doubt of the new technology. Viable demonstrators also help with this aim.

Working through a group such as an Alvey Community Club can be a very good strategy. Strength in numbers is cost effective and builds a critical mass not otherwise obtainable. There is still a need, however, for those involved to take firm, confident action to establish the project, whether at Club or Company level.

How the project originated

The ABI, the Association of British Insurers, is the trade body for the UK Insurance Industry. An initiative at the ABI, begun in 1984, connected with the Alvey IKBS awareness programme, and the Club was built from there.

Other features were the early involvement of Logica as system builder, and the establishment of a good Club administration at the Insurance Technical Bureau (ITB). (The administration was later transferred to City University, when the ITB closed down in early 1986.)

Motivation and background

The stirrings of commercial interest in expert systems have been present for some time now, probably at least since the announcement of the Japanese Fifth Generation Initiative in 1981. However, there has been a relative lack of company confidence to justify a start in the field for any individual company.

The Alvey awareness programme, with its vehicle of the IKBS Community Clubs, has therefore filled a gap. It has been the stimulus into action for many in the commercial sector, and certainly for the insurance companies.

How funding and approval were obtained

In the Aries member companies, DP departments tended to push the project forward rather than system users.

Each company contributed £10 000, which brought in an eventual total of £230 000 to the project. At Alvey, the project was accepted for the Community Club programme, and £125 000 was allocated.

How the project was managed

The project was governed by a Steering Committee of eight company members, two academics and an Alvey Officer. The detailed project management was carried out by Logica. A standard project structure was applied, both in handling personnel and in the phasing of the project.

Two members of the Steering Committee were appointed as Technical Coordinators to maintain close links with the project team, particularly in the periods between Committee meetings. A permanent secretary was also appointed to handle the Club's organization. With 30 Club members to look after, and with workshops, committees and Club meetings happening at the rate of at least two per month overall, this proved to be a non-trivial role.

Support from top management

The low entry cost to the project—£10 000 in all, or £5 000 pa—meant that top management decisions were not needed in order for a company to take up Club membership. There was, however, increasing interest and support from higher management as the results became apparent.

Timescales

The original plan for a 16 month project expanded to 21 months. The essential reason for this was the complexity of Equity Selection, which turned out on detailed study to be much greater than originally anticipated. The additional finance needed was by this time available, since more companies (23 in all) joined the project than initially expected.

The importance of the application to the organization

Both underwriting and investment are vital tasks within insurance. Fire insurance is one of the staple activities of the industry, and investment returns have a crucial effect on the overall profitability. Expert systems in both of these areas can enable competitive edge to be gained and/or maintained.

Preservation of expertise within the company when an investment or underwriting expert retires or leaves is also a relevant advantage.

Tactical as opposed to strategic

In their present state, both Aries systems have a tactical rather than a strategic role. They are currently being taken on board as such by the companies. Further development of the systems should, however, in time point the way towards strategic advantage.

The reason for using the AI approach

Neither of the Aries systems could be produced cost-effectively by conventional techniques. Full procedural coding of the applications plus updating of the knowledge bases would take too long to achieve.

The influence of peer group pressure on the decision to adopt AI

We are not aware of any such pressure. The whole development was conceived as an AI/expert system exercise by definition.

Initial gain of AI knowledge by the organization

Aries essentially gained its knowledge from Logica, although a few members did have a little earlier experience of the field. Logica had been involved in AI for 5 years and more at the start of the project, particularly through its Cambridge Research Group.

Envisagement of maintenance of knowledge base

Fire risks

In this field, the parameters are slow-moving, though KB maintenance will still be vital. One point is that the system should free the time of the top experts for dealing with this task.

The existing position is that companies use various rate books with their tabular variations. These books have to be maintained in any case, so that an underwriting expert system is no different in this respect.

Equity selection

To begin with, tuning the Aries system to the practice of particular companies and even to individual experts within a company is necessary.

Continuous updating of the KB will be needed, since investment is a fast-moving field. Indeed, KB maintenance for investment systems will be a very significant problem area. Testing difficulties in particular are likely to be experienced, and the full answer requires further work.

LESSONS LEARNED

Reasons for success

The Aries Club was fortunate in having a good, competent team with all-round abilities, both in the technical and management areas. Logica's depth of experience in systems building was a very significant factor—a disciplined approach to project management enabled ambitious targets to be both established and achieved.

The Club was fortunate to find experts who were highly skilled in their fields and who cooperated fully in the knowledge elicitation. Overall, a good, cooperative spirit prevailed between Club members throughout the life of the Club.

The Club's choice of hardware and software proved to be appropriate at all stages. There was good support from suppliers, especially Unisys (Sperry) who provided the Explorer and Kee.

The major bottlenecks

The details of the Club Rules and Collaboration Agreement, on which the enterprise was founded, proved tiresome to sort out.

The process of actually obtaining money from Alvey, even once it had been properly approved, was little short of a nightmare. The difficulty did not, however, stem from the Alvey Directorate itself, whose officers did everything they possibly could for the Club. The real problems lay in the DTI procedures for grant payment, which are ill-adapted for dealing with non-standard initiatives. It is another case of new and vital initiatives (i.e. Alvey) being disadvantaged by outdated bureaucratic procedures.

In Equity Selection, the availability of experts and system users (who were experts in any case) was a problem. Given the pressures of work in modern-day investment, this is hardly surprising. The only solution was to prepare very carefully for the expert interviews, and to tailor the depth of the system to the time available for knowledge elicitation.

The testing of systems generally was a problem—the Club did not have adequate resources to pursue system testing to a satisfactory level. Again, expert availability for this purpose was a serious bottleneck.

How principled were the decisions described above

Decisions were made on a pragmatic basis throughout. Running a project such as Aries depends on doing what is possible and mutually agreeable at each stage, rather than what is ideal.

The criteria used were: cost, usability, practical delivery of systems, timescales—all of which are thoroughly commercial considerations. (One possible exception to this is work put in during the project to illustrate variations in user interfaces and control structures.)

PERSONAL COMMENTS

Gary Chamberlin

We all learned a lot—about expert systems, about the problems surrounding their practical application in industry, about how to run a collaborative project. As a result of the work, the UK Insurance Industry has started out on the road towards taking AI seriously, and seeking its tangible commercial benefits.

Richard Lelliott

An exciting and occasionally frustrating project, with a satisfying and satisfactory conclusion. The cost effectiveness of the 'club' philosophy has been proven, and industry helped another step along the IT path.

CONCLUSIONS

The Aries initiative has been a success by any standards. All the original objectives have been surpassed, and the insurance industry has been given an excellent base of examples on which to build. We also found that the commercial drive of business members contributed more to the ultimate success of the project than academic zeal, perhaps because of the financial stake.

The two most successful areas of the project should be singled out for special mention. Knowledge acquisition, from being shrouded in myths and misunderstanding, is now more fully understood by the Club members. A way ahead can be explored by them with confidence, using paper models (intermediate representations). Secondly, the PC shells, so long the poor relation of the expert system world, gained acceptance during the final stage of Aries, as slow and expensive stand-alone machinery was replaced by cost effective and fast delivery environments.

BIBLIOGRAPHY

Butler, A.R. and Chamberlin, G. F. (1988). The Aries Club—Experience of Expert Systems in Insurance and Investment. In D.S. Moralee (ed.), *Research and Development in Expert Systems IV*, Cambridge University Press.

Chamberlin, G.F. (1989). The Aries Club—Practical Work in Insurance Expert Systems. In D. Shillito (ed.), *IT—A Strategic Guide for the UK Insurance Industry*, IBC Financial Technology Publishing, Byfleet.

Chamberlin, G.F., Neale, I.M. and Khan, M.N. (1989). TULIP: Life Underwriting Expert System. In N. Shadbolt (ed.), *Research and Development in Expert Systems VI*, Cambridge University Press.

Note: The detailed Aries work 1985–87 is described in the series of Club reports produced by Logica on Stages 1–5 of the project. These are confidential to Club members, and cannot be released under the terms of the Club confidentiality agreement.

10

KARDIO: An Expert System for ECG Interpretation

Ivan Bratko, Nada Lavrač and Igor Mozetič

ABSTRACT

KARDIO is an expert system for the electrocardiographic (ECG) diagnosis of cardiac arrhythmias. The system features deep and shallow knowledge. The qualitative model of the heart represents deep-level knowledge about the electrical activity of the heart and its possible disorders, known as cardiac arrhythmias. By means of qualitative simulation on all possible combinations of heart disorders the model was compiled into the surface ECG interpretation knowledge base consisting of an exhaustive set of arrhythmia–ECG relations. Using inductive learning tools the arrhythmia–ECG base was compressed into the form of surface-level rules that can be used for efficient diagnosis and prediction of arrhythmias.

INTRODUCTION

KARDIO is a medical expert system for the electrocardiographic (ECG) diagnosis of disorders in the heart, known as cardiac arrhythmias. This expert task is based on the interpretation of ECGs, i.e. recordings of electrical signals generated by the heart muscle. The system was developed by the collaboration of researchers of the Artificial Intelligence Laboratory, Computer Science Department at the Jožef Stefan Institute and cardiologists of the Center for Intensive Internal Medicine at the University Medical Center in Ljubljana, Yugoslavia.

At the start of the project in 1982 our plan was to develop an expert system for the diagnosis and treatment of cardiac arrhythmias from complete clinical and ECG data. In the development of a prototype diagnostic expert system (Bratko *et al* 1982) it became obvious that the ECG interpretation knowledge is the most important for diagnosis of heart disorders and that it is necessary to consider that there can be several disorders simultaneously present in the heart. The large number of potentially possible combinations of disorders made it impossible to acquire the ECG interpretation knowledge by direct encoding of rules in interaction with medical specialists. Therefore we approached the problem of multiple arrhythmias by constructing a deep, logical model of the electrical heart activity. The adequate representational form for the physiological model of the heart was that of qualitative descriptions, expressed in a logic language and not the traditional quantitative representation. The deep qualitative model was then used as a generator of diagnostic rules.

By automatic transformations from the logical model of the heart three surface operational knowledge bases were derived. The knowledge base for the ECG interpretation of arrhythmias consisting of an exhaustive set of arrhythmia–ECG relations was compiled from the qualitative model by the breadth-first simulation of all mathematically possible combinations of heart disorders. This surface representation facilitates fast ECG diagnosis, but is rather complex in terms of memory space (over 5 MB, stored as text file). Therefore, using inductive learning tools, the arrhythmia–ECG base was compressed into the form of rules used for efficient computer diagnosis and prediction of arrhythmias. The induced diagnostic and prediction rules are compact and similar to the knowledge found in medical literature and used by experts. The described transformations of knowledge are shown in Figure 10.1. A detailed description of these transformations is found in Bratko *et al* (1988, 1989).

We consider KARDIO in its present form a success as a study

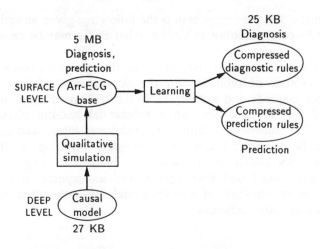

Figure 10.1. Deep and surface levels of cardiological knowledge and transformations between representations

into knowledge acquisition for expert systems by means of qualitative modelling and machine learning, rather than as an operational expert system routinely used in medical practice. The obstacles to routine use of KARDIO are analysed later. One problem is that KARDIO does not accept an actual ECG trace, but requires that the patient's ECG be symbolically described by the user. The obvious way to overcome this would be to connect KARDIO to an existing ECG analysis machine. Such machines accept ECG traces and perform low-level signal analysis resulting in symbolic descriptions required by KARDIO. KARDIO could then not only be used to interpret the extracted features, but also to guide, by the deep model, the low level feature extraction process. This would make feature extraction in ECG analysis machines more reliable than it is at present.

OBJECTIVES

The main goal of the project was to build an expert system for efficient ECG diagnosis and prediction of multiple cardiac arrhythmias. The diagnosis task can be stated as follows: given an ECG, what arrhythmias could have caused it, i.e. what heart disorders are indicated by given

ECG features. The prediction task is the following: given an arrhythmia, what are its corresponding ECGs, i.e. what ECGs may be caused by a given heart disorder.

Besides this initial goal we wanted to use this complex medical domain also as a source of problems for the development of new artificial intelligence methods and techniques. In KARDIO qualitative modelling was used for the first time on a substantial real-life physiological problem. The 'knowledge acquisition cycle' was introduced consisting of automatic transformations of knowledge, resulting in the form of compact operational rules. Further, a hierarchical organization of a qualitative model was investigated, and an experiment completed whereby the construction of a deep model was automated by means of machine learning techniques.

SYSTEM SPECIFICATION

The specification of the system KARDIO is the following. First, build an expert system for the ECG diagnosis of cardiac arrhythmias that accepts a symbolic ECG description and finds the arrhythmias which correspond to the given ECG. Second, build a prediction expert system that accepts an arrhythmia and finds the corresponding ECG descriptions that may be caused by the arrhythmia. The specification omits the method for knowledge acquisition and the formalism for knowledge representation, these will be dealt with in later sections.

The above specification is based on the assumption that each electrocardiogram can be described in terms of symbolic features that are indicative of a diagnosis, such as the rate or the shape of the QRS complex of the heart beat. In KARDIO as well as in medical literature ECG features are of a qualitative, rather than quantitative nature. A specification of such features for a given ECG is called a qualitative ECG description. The following is an example of an ECG description that consists of values assigned to qualitative ECG attributes.

> [rhythm_QRS = irregular] &
> [dominant_P = abnormal] &
> [rate_of_P = between_100_250] &
> [relation_P_QRS = after_P_some_ QRS_miss] &
> [dominant_PR = prolonged] &
> [dominant_QRS = normal] &
> [rate_of_QRS = between_60_100 V between_100_250]

The language for the qualitative ECG description consists of seven attributes for the description of regular heart beats. For each type of ectopic beat another triple of attributes is added. Each of the attributes has from two to seven possible values. The system deals with the set of 30 simple arrhythmias and all their combinations.

The above specification is somewhat unrealistic from the practical point of view, as it specifies that KARDIO accept as input a symbolic ECG description rather than an actual ECG signal. This limitation could be avoided by integrating KARDIO with an ECG analysis machine which would automate the translation from the actual ECG signal to its symbolic description.

ORGANIZATIONAL ISSUES AND USE OF RESOURCES

The project was started as a research project of the Artificial Intelligence Laboratory, Computer Science Department at the Jožef Stefan Institute in Ljubljana in 1982. As a research project, it was conducted much in a typical 'academic style' with rather flexible organization. Much of the work was done also by research students. The researchers who contributed most to the project were Ivan Bratko, Igor Mozetič and Nada Lavrač. The project was continuously supported by the Research Community of Slovenia. Additional support came from: the European Economic Community within the COST-13 project Artificial Intelligence and Pattern Recognition, Fulbright Foundation, National Science Foundation, Office of Naval Research, Defense Advanced Research Project Agency and US Army Research Institute for the Behavioral and Social Sciences through its European Science Coordination Office.

Using dialogue-based techniques for knowledge acquisition, our initial experiments resulted in a small rule-based expert system for diagnosis of arrhythmias from clinical and ECG data (Bratko et al 1982, Zrimec et al 1983) and an expert system for the treatment of arrhythmias (Klemenc, et al 1984). The work was done in collaboration with researchers of the Faculty of Electrical Engineering and medical students of the E Kardelj University in Ljubljana.

The version of the model essentially the same as the present version was developed in the MSc Thesis by Mozetič (1984). The derived knowledge base for the ECG interpretation of arrhythmias consisting of an exhaustive set of arrhythmia–ECG relations was used in an expert system for ECG diagnosis of cardiac arrhythmias KARDIO-E (Lavrač et *al* 1985) developed in the MSc Thesis by Lavrač (1984). At this stage there was a number of students involved in the development of a system for graphical representation of ECG curves and for schematical representation of the states of the heart.

Using an inductive learning program of the AQ family the arrhythmia–ECG base was compressed into the form of rules used for efficient computer diagnosis and prediction of arrhythmias (Mozetič 1986; Mozetič *et al* 1984; Bratko *et al* 1988,1989). A further research result was the development of a qualitative model acquisition system that, by using machine learning techniques, supports the semi-automatic top-down development of qualitative models (Mozetič 1987a,b, Bratko *et al* 1989). Most of this work was done as Mozetič's PhD Thesis (Mozetič 1988) during his leave of absence at the University of Illinois at Urbana-Champaign.

During the project different hardware resources were available. The work started using DEC 10 and was continued on different VAX and SUN machines, and IBM PCs. The main software tool was Prolog that has served both as a prototyping tool and as the implementation language for our products such as the model of the heart and the ECG diagnosis system KARDIO-E. A version of the diagnosis system was developed in Pascal. Prolog was also used in the development of the qualitative model acquisition system. Other main development tools were the inductive programs for learning from examples such as NEWGEM (Mozetič 1985), a version of the AQ learning system (Michalski 1969, Michalski *et al* 1986).

INVOLVEMENT OF DOMAIN SPECIALISTS

KARDIO was developed in collaboration with cardiologists Matija Horvat, Bojan Čerček, Anton Grad and Primož Rode of the Center for Intensive Internal Medicine at the University Medical Center in Ljubljana. They were strongly involved in the initial design of the system, in the development of the initial diagnostic system using dialogue-based techniques and in the debugging of the logical model of the heart. Other medical doctors—general practitioners—were involved in the assessment of the correctness and the practical usefulness of the rule-based diagnostic system. Matija Horvat, Peter Macfarlane of the Western Royal Infirmary, Glasgow, and G. van Herpen of University Hospital, Leiden, participated as medical specialists in the evaluation of the KARDIO knowledge base.

KNOWLEDGE ACQUISITION

The project KARDIO illustrates how the qualitative modelling approach and machine learning technology, characteristic of second generation expert systems, can be used to construct knowledge bases whose complexity is far beyond the complexity of traditional, dialogue-based techniques for knowledge acquisition. The KARDIO knowledge acquisition paradigm, named the 'knowledge acquisition cycle', is illustrated in Figure 10.2.

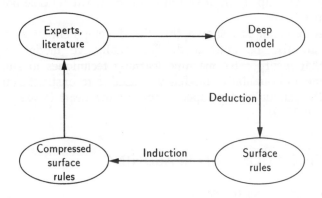

Figure 10.2 The KARDIO knowledge acquisition cycle

Initially, the deep qualitative model of the heart was developed manually from medical literature and in consultation with medical specialists. Three surface operational knowledge bases were derived by automatic transformations from the original model. Details of these transformations are explained later. The ECG interpretation knowledge base consisting of an exhaustive set of arrhythmia–ECG relations was compiled from the qualitative model by the simulation of all mathematically possible combinations of heart disorders. This transformation corresponds to the deduction step in Figure 10.2. Using inductive learning tools the arrhythmia–ECG base was compressed into the form of rules used for efficient computer diagnosis and prediction of arrhythmias. These two transformations correspond to the induction step in Figure 10.2.

The comparison between the original human codifications and the generated compressed representation offers a powerful possibility for knowledge validation. Differences between the original human codification and a compressed representation can result from either an error in compressed representation, or a slip in the human codification. In the former case, the error is the consequence of an error in the deep model since both the deductive and the inductive derivation steps in Figure 10.2 are truth preserving. Thus in this case the knowledge acquisition cycle provides a feedback loop for verifying and correcting the deep model. In the latter case, a slip in the human codification, the knowledge acquisition cycle will expose blemishes in the existing, original expert formulations and may thus help to improve those. In the KARDIO case both effects were noticed.

Further research has shown that the development of a qualitative model can also be automated. The qualitative model acquisition system that incorporates machine learning techniques to support the development of qualitative models was used to reconstruct a substantial part of the manually developed model of the heart (Mozetič 1987a,b, Bratko *et al* 1989).

REPRESENTATION AND REASONING

Qualitative model of the heart

The deep qualitative model of the electrical activity of the heart specifies causal relationships between objects and events in the heart. These include electrical impulses, ECG signals, impulse generation, impulse conduction and summation. The model can be thought of as an electric network as shown in Figure 10.3. However, signals that propagate in this network are represented qualitatively by symbolic descriptions rather than quantitatively by voltage against time relations.

Known approaches to qualitative modelling such as Kuipers (1986), de Kleer and Brown (1984) and Forbus (1984), were applied to qualitative physics where a classical model, expressed by a set of differential equations is usually known. In contrast, we were concerned with problems where a classical model does not exist or is too complicated to be expressed by the type of constraints used in these approaches.

In our approach we formalize constraints in logic and adopt the reductionists' view to qualitative modelling in which the behaviour of a model can be derived solely from its structure and behaviour of its components (de Kleer and Brown 1983). A qualitative model is thus defined by its structure (a set of components and their connections)

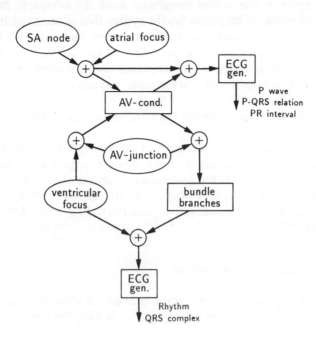

Figure 10.3   Model of the heart as a network composed of impulse generators, conduction paths, impulse summators and ECG generators

and functions of individual components. The ingredients of the model of the heart are the following:

(1) nodes of the network are impulse generators, conduction pathways, impulse summators and ECG generators;

(2) dictionary of simple arrhythmias related to heart disorders;

(3) 'legality' constraints over the states of the heart that recognize certain categories of states that are rejected by the model as 'illegal';

(4) 'local' rules that specify the behaviour of individual components of the heart in the presence of various abnormal states;

(5) 'global' rules that define causal relations between impulse generators and conduction pathways in the heart, electrical impulses and ECG features.

All the rules in the model essentially have the syntax of first-order predicate calculus, more precisely, the syntax that is accepted by Prolog under the Edinburgh notational conventions (Pereira *et al* 1978).

Rules are composed of subexpressions in specialized languages for describing the state of the heart, impulses that are conducted through the heart, and ECG patterns. For example, the term

heart(atr_focus: permanent(regular, between_100_250))

is a partial specification of the state of the heart. It says that the atrial focus is discharging permanent impulses (as opposed to occasional) with a regular rhythm at the tachycardic rate (i.e. somewhere between 100 and 250). Each statement about the state of the heart specifies the functional state of a component of the heart (the atrial focus in the example above).

Qualitative simulation algorithm

Formally, the qualitative simulation consists of theorem proving and theorem generation. Although the global rules have the syntax of Prolog, they are not directly executed by Prolog's own interpreting mechanism. The main reason is the need for additional control to improve executional efficiency. Thus the qualitative simulation is done by a special rule-interpreter implemented in Prolog.

Each simulation run consists of the following steps:

(1) Instantiate the model by a given arrhythmia, using the definitions of arrhythmias in terms of the heart disorders.

(2) Check the resulting functional state of the heart against the legality constraints (logical, physiological, medically interesting).

(3) Execute the model by triggering the rules until a state is reached in which no rule fires (this process is combinatorial due to the non-deterministic nature of the heart's components).

(4) Collect the proved assertions about ECG and then construct an ECG description that corresponds to the given arrhythmia.

The complex part above is step 3. It is based on the forward chaining of global rules in the model. The simulator starts with some initial database of facts (initially these just specify the state of the heart) and then keeps firing the global rules until no more rules can fire. The constraint here is that no rule is repeatedly executed on the same piece of information. Execution of rules generates new assertions that are added into the database. These new assertions are regarded as hypotheses that can later be proved false, which causes backtracking. Backtracking to a previous point occurs when the current content of the database is found inconsistent, i.e. some assertion has been generated which leads to contradiction.

Implementation of the simulation algorithm

The easiest way of implementing the simulation algorithm outlined above is to use depth-first search. This is straightforward and suitable for single simulation runs, that is for answering questions of the prediction type: given an arrhythmia, what are its corresponding ECGs. If several ECGs are possible, they are simply generated through backtracking. Also, an execution trace obtained in such a simulation run can be used as the basis for generating an explanation of what is going on in the heart. This is suitable since the simulation steps follow the causal chains of events in the heart, according to the global rules of the model. These rules essentially describe the causal relations between objects and events in the heart.

In a Prolog implementation of depth-first simulation on various machines, ranging from Edinburgh Prolog on DEC 10 (Pereira *et al* 1978) to Arity Prolog on IBM PC/XT/AT (Arity 1986), each simulation run takes a few CPU seconds, producing all alternative ECGs.

This straightforward method, however, is not as effective in answering questions of the diagnostic type. Diagnostic-type questions are of the form: given an ECG, what arrhythmias could have caused it? To answer such questions, we could run the model in the opposite direction. Start with a given ECG and end with possible functional states of the heart that may cause this ECG.

We can in fact run the model in this direction by the backward chaining of the rules in the model. In order to do that we can reverse the global rules and use the simple depth-first search again. However, the practical problem of efficiency now arises because the branching factor ('non-determinism') in the backward direction is much higher than that in the forward direction. This entails much more backtracking and rather complex search, thus rendering this approach to diagnosis impractical. Efficiency can be improved by rewriting the model so as to introduce more constraints into the rules, which would help the system recognize contradictive branches at an earlier stage. An attempt at reformulating rules, however, revealed two drawbacks. The size of the model increases considerably, and the transparency is greatly affected. This, in turn, mars the explanation of the heart's behaviour based on the execution trace.

An alternative way to achieve efficient diagnosis is to compile the model. That is to generate from the deep model of the heart a complete surface level representation of the arrhythmia–ECG relation (Figure 10.1) as a set of pairs of the form:

(Combined_arrhythmia, ECG_description)

In principle this can be done by executing the depth-first simulation (forward chaining) for each possible combined arrhythmia, and storing all its ECG manifestations. It would be necessary to repeat this for all possible alternative execution paths in order to obtain all possible ECGs for each arrhythmia. This is again rather inefficient for two reasons. First, for each disjunctive solution the simulator has to backtrack to some previously used rule in the model and restore its previous state. Second, the final resulting ECG descriptions have the form of disjunctions of terms about ECG. These disjunctive terms can be more complex than necessary and can be simplified later. This posterior simplification, however, is again a complex operation. Each disjunct is the result of an alternative execution path. The simplification can be carried out much more economically at the very moment that a disjunct (or, typically, part of it) is generated, before it gets further expanded and mixed in the expression with other not closely related terms.

These two factors (saving the restoration of previous states, and immediate simplification of disjunctive expressions) motivated the implementation of another type of simulation algorithm that handles alternative execution paths in a breadth-first fashion. This algorithm develops alternatives essentially in parallel and currently simplifies disjunctions. The simplification rules actually used were rather model dependent in the sense that they do not preserve logical equivalence in general but only in the special case of the properties of the heart model. So the 'breadth-first' simulation is not general and we would possibly have to modify the simplification rules in the case of a change in the model.

Compilation of deep model into surface representation

The breadth-first simulation algorithm was executed on all mathematically possible combinations of simple arrhythmias. The majority of these combined arrhythmias were eliminated by the legality constraints over the states of the heart. The complete arrhythmia–ECG knowledge base was thus automatically generated which corresponds to the deduction step in Figure 10.2. Results of the generation reveal some interesting points. The most complicated arrhythmias are combinations of seven simple disorders. There are altogether 2419 'legal' combined arrhythmias within the level of detail of the heart model. These arrhythmias are related to the large number of 140966 generated ECG manifestations. This is indicative of the difficulty in ECG diagnosis of cardiac arrhythmias. On average, each arrhythmia has almost 60 different corresponding ECG manifestations. The relation between arrhythmias and their ECG manifestations is represented by 8314 Prolog clauses generated as a result of the compilation of the deep model into its surface representation. Each clause represents a pair: (Combined_arrhythmia, ECG_description). Each ECG description specifies a number of possible ECGs, about 20 on average. This is the reduction factor due to the simplification technique used in the breadth-first simulation.

The set of 140966 ECG patterns (the right-hand sides of the arrhythmia–ECG rules) are not unique. The same ECG patterns can occur at several places which means that several arrhythmias can have the same ECG manifestation. Consequently, arrhythmias cannot be unambiguously diagnosed from a given ECG. Empirical probing showed that for a given ECG there are typically between two and four possible combined arrhythmias in the arrhythmia knowledge base. From the medical point of view, however, these alternative diagnoses are not significantly different from the point of view of treatment. They would typically all require the same treatment.

The arrhythmia–ECG base generated from the model is complete in two ways. First, it comprises all physiologically possible arrhythmias at the level of detail of the model. Second, each arrhythmia is associated with all its possible ECG manifestations. In principle, the problem of diagnosing is now simple. As the rules in the knowledge base are logical implications, we can apply the *modus tollens* rule of inference on them. Consider a rule of the form

Combined_arrhythmia $\Rightarrow$ ECG_description

where ECG_description is the disjunction of all possible ECGs that Combined_arrhythmia can cause. Then, if a given ECG does not match ECG_description it follows that Combined_arrhythmia is eliminated as a diagnostic possibility. All arrhythmias that are not thus eliminated are possible diagnoses with respect to the given ECG data. Any further discrimination between the so obtained set of arrhythmias can be done only on the basis of some additional evidence (e.g. clinical data). Also, as the knowledge base is complete (with respect to the level of detail in the model) the empty set of possible arrhythmias would imply that the given ECG is physiologically impossible.

Compression of the arrhythmia–ECG base using inductive learning tools

As discussed, the arrhythmia–ECG base can be used for efficient ECG diagnosis based on a simple pattern-matching rule. However, it is rather bulky for some practical application requirements. If stored as a text file, the 8314 Prolog clauses that represent the arrhythmia–ECG relation, occupy more than 5 MB of store. Also this mere complexity renders the contents of this knowledge base difficult to compare with the conventional medical codifications of the electrocardiographic knowledge. Therefore an attempt was made to find a more compact representation of the arrhythmia–ECG base that would still allow efficient ECG diagnosis. This corresponds to the induction step in the knowledge-acquisition cycle of Figure 10.2.

The main idea was to use the compiled representation as a source of examples and to use an inductive learning program to obtain their compact descriptions. Various inductive learning programs were used for this purpose, all of them belonging to the AQ family of learning programs (e.g. Michalski 1969, Michalski et al 1986). The final results were obtained with NEWGEM (Mozetič 1985). With the complete arrhythmia–ECG base as the set of examples, the number of examples for these learning programs would be too high. Therefore we had first to generate a subset of the knowledge base that would retain its completeness to the greatest possible extent. Some domain-specific factorization properties facilitated the selection of a considerably reduced subset for learning whereby the information thus lost can be recovered by a small set of additional rules. The subset thus obtained was substantially smaller than the original arrhythmia–ECG base. There are 943 combined arrhythmias and 5240 ECGs in the subset compared to 2419 arrhythmias and 140 966 ECGs in the complete knowledge base.

Roughly, the compression procedure was as follows: The learning subset of the arrhythmia–ECG base comprised 943 rules (corresponding to 943 combined arrhythmias) of the form

Combined_arrhythmia $\Rightarrow$ ECG_description

The goal of learning was to convert this information into rules of two forms

(1) Compressed prediction rules that answer the question: What ECGs may be caused by a given disorder in a heart's component?

(2) Compressed diagnostic rules that answer the question: What heart disorders are indicated by a given ECG feature?

Learning programs of the the AQ family generate class descriptions as VL1 expressions (Variable-Valued Logic 1, Michalski and Larson 1975). Before such programs could have been used, the learning subset had to be converted into rules of yet two other forms in order to get the right input for the learning programs required, i.e. examples of objects that belong to classes being learned. For synthesizing prediction rules, the proper starting point were pairs of the form

(Selected_disorder, ECG_description)

where a 'selected disorder' is for example: atrial focus is in the tachycardic state. For the learning program, the disorder is the class, and the ECG description is the vector of attribute values.

The starting point for the synthesis of diagnostic rules were pairs of the form

(Selected_ECG_feature, Combined_arrhythmia)

where a 'selected ECG feature' is for example: P wave has abnormal shape.

In general, rules of these forms are not logically equivalent to the original rules, so they have to be used with care. Conditions under which both the original rules and the transformed ones produce equivalent diagnostic results have to be verified in the case of this transformation (Mozetič 1986, Bratko et al 1989).

Figure 10.1 shows the compression effects achieved in terms of storage space needed when storing different representations simply as text files. The figure 25 KB associated with the corresponding representations includes both the induced descriptions plus the extra rules needed to attain logical equivalence with the exhaustive arrhythmia–ECG representation. Notice the compression factor of about 200. The similarity in size between the deep model and the compressed representations is incidental.

[av conduct = avb3] ⇒
[rhythm_QRS = regular] &
[relation_P_QRS = independent_P_QRS]

Goldman (1976): In this condition the atria and ventricles beat entirely independently of one another. The ventricular rhythm is usually quite regular but at much slower rate (20–60).

Phibbs (1973): 1. The atrial and ventricular rates are different: the atrial rate is faster; the ventricular rate is slow and regular. 2. There is no consistent relation between P waves and QRS complexes.

Figure 10.4 A synthesized prediction rule (above) and some corresponding descriptions from the medical literature

Figure 10.4 shows a prediction rule generated by the induction algorithms and some corresponding descriptions from the medical literature. Some of the synthesized descriptions correspond very well to the descriptions in the medical literature, as Figure 10.4 illustrates. On the other hand, some of the synthesized descriptions are considerably more complex than those in the medical literature. The computer generated descriptions in such cases give much more detailed specification which may not be necessary for an intelligent reader with the physiological background. Such a reader can usually infer the missing detail from his or her background knowledge. However, the additional details must still be made explicit in the case of a computer application in the form of a diagnostic expert system. Otherwise a lot of background knowledge and inference would have to be added which would be extremely difficult and its correctness hard to verify.

Here is an example of a synthesized diagnostic rule:

[relation_P_QRS = after_P_some_QRS_miss] ⇒
[av_conduct = wen V mob2]
V
[atr_focus = afl V af] & [av_conduct = normal]

This rule corresponds to a particular diagnostic feature in the ECG, characterized by the feature that some P waves are not followed (as normally) by the corresponding QRS complexes. The rule states that this feature is indicative of the defects called Wenckebach or Mobitz 2, or, when the AV conductance is normal, of the atrial flutter or fibrillation. The rule thus clearly indicates what kinds of disorders a diagnostic system should be looking for in the case that this abnormality is detected in the ECG.

Quantitative summary

In KARDIO, various representations of the ECG knowledge are used. The main three representations are at different knowledge levels:

— deep level: the qualitative causal model of the heart

— surface level: the complete arrhythmia–ECG base

— surface level compressed: compact diagnostic and prediction rules.

Table 10.1 compares these representations from the following points of view:

— nature of knowledge
— method of construction
— representational formalism
— size as text file (in kilobytes)
— direction of inference the representation supports
— the functional role.

Table 10.1 Comparison of different representations of electrocardiographic knowledge

	I Causal model of the heart	II Arrhythmia-ECG base	III Compressed diagnostic knowledge
Nature of knowledge	deep causal	surface operational	surface operational
Method of construction	manual	automatic synthesis from I	automatic compression from II
Representational formalism	first-order logic	propositional logic	propositional logic
Size	27 KB	5 MB	25 KB
Direction of inference	Arr $\Rightarrow$ ECG forward	Arr $\Leftrightarrow$ ECG both	Arr $\Leftarrow$ ECG backward
Role	qualitative simulation, generate II	diagnosis, provide examples for III	diagnosis

The size of the compressed diagnostic knowledge of 25 KB accounts for both the compressed rules plus some necessary additional information. The compressed rules themselves are not sufficient for the diagnosis because of loss of information in the selection of the learning subset of the arrhythmia–ECG base. To attain the full diagnostic equivalence with the arrhythmia–ECG knowledge base we have to add descriptions of arrhythmias and ECG features that were eliminated in selecting the learning subset. Furthermore, 'legality' constraints and related testing procedures have to be included as well. After adding all of these, the size of the compressed diagnostic knowledge becomes 25 KB.

USER INTERFACE

KARDIO consists of several subsystems using the various forms of the ECG interpretation knowledge (see the different knowledge bases also in Figure 10.1). Here we describe the user interface of the KARDIO-E expert system for ECG diagnosis of cardiac arrhythmias (Lavrač *et al* 1985). Its menu-driven communication module leads the user when choosing among the functions of the system. We only mention the most important functions of the system, namely the input of the patient's ECG data, diagnosis, explanation and teaching about arrhythmias.

Normally, the user first enters the patient's ECG data. The user is helped by the system's queries for specifying for each attribute its value from a menu of all its possible values. For an attribute the user can select also the value 'unknown'. User's choice of this value is interpreted as if all the values for the attribute were possible (so no arrhythmia gets eliminated on the basis of this attribute). Once the patient's ECG has been specified the user may request the diagnosis.

If the system's diagnosis contradicts the user's opinion he/she can ask the system for an explanation why a certain diagnosis (the one that he/she considers to be correct) was excluded. The system then outputs the values of attributes which eliminated the user's hypothesis from the set of possible arrhythmias. If such an arrhythmia is even theoretically impossible regardless of the patient's ECG, the explanation consists of those constraints in the model of the heart that eliminated the arrhythmia from the initial set of all candidate diagnoses.

The teaching function generates problems for the user so that a user is asked to interpret a randomly chosen ECG description. This function is supported by a graphic facility for generating and displaying of ECG curves. These ECG diagrams are synthetically generated from their ECG description. Figure 10.5 shows an example.

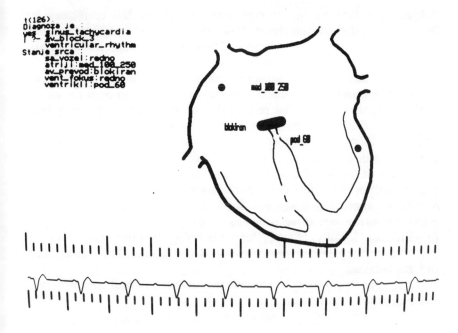

Figure 10.5   The graphics facility in KARDIO: a schematic illustration of the heart failures and an automatically generated ECG signal (below) that corresponds to this arrhythmia (in this case the arrhythmia is the combination of sinus tachycardia, av block 3 and ventricular rhythm)

EVALUATION OF COMPLETENESS AND CLINICAL APPLICABILITY

In an assessment study of KARDIO (Grad and Čerček 1984), cardiologists made the following estimates based on clinical tests of KARDIO described below: the knowledge base covers 90 to 95% of patients in a population suffering from cardiac arrhythmias. In a 'selected' population (specially difficult cases referred to a specialist cardiologist on account of previous examinations) KARDIO would correctly handle 75% of arrhythmia cases. Here 'correct handling' means that KARDIO's diagnosis would imply correct treatment. In an actual test with KARDIO-E (the version of KARDIO used in this assessment study) on 36 randomly selected arrhythmia cases from internal medical practice the arrhythmia knowledge base was sufficient in 34 cases (94%). The failed cases are due to some incompleteness of the deep model, such as the present model's incapability of handling artificial pacemakers.

Another validation study was made to assess the correctness of the deep model of the heart (and thus also the derived surface representations). For this purpose a subset of 105 combined arrhythmias was selected from the complete set of 2419 arrhythmias in the arrhythmia–ECG base. The subset was selected randomly in a way to best represent the complete problem domain with respect to both the nature of the arrhythmias and the complexity of arrhythmias, ranging from simple disorders up to most complex combinations of seven disorders. Of course, this selection does not in any way correspond to statistical distribution of cases in the medical practice.

For each of the selected arrhythmias, a form was prepared containing one of the possible ECG descriptions associated with this arrhythmia. Additional alternative diagnoses of the same ECG were also given. The evaluating cardiologists were then asked to comment on these diagnoses. To minimize locality effects, three cardiologists from three different countries participated in the evaluation (Great Britain, The Netherlands, and Yugoslavia).

The following paragraphs summarize the most critical conclusions of this evaluation experiment:

(1) The knowledge content was assessed as correct, although there were several specialists' comments mainly prompted by misinterpretation of particular features in the ECG description language and variations in the medical terminology.

(2) The ECG description language can be improved to alleviate terminological problems referred to above. (Concrete suggestions were implemented in a later version of the heart model.)

(3) The level of detail in the heart model could be more suitably balanced for practical application. In some respects the present model is unnecessarily detailed whereas it would be useful to cover a few additional disorders, although there was no general agreement among the cardiologists on this question.

(4) The changes in the description language and the fine adjustments in the level of detail can be easily introduced within the present framework. All the representation formalisms, associated algorithms and programs can be used without change.

The problems mentioned above eventually made it difficult to obtain from this validation study any significant quantitative results regarding the completeness and correctness of the KARDIO model.

In respect of clinical application of KARDIO, the cardiologists felt that a significant limitation is that KARDIO accepts as input symbolic ECG descriptions rather than the actual ECG signal. Thus the user is at present required to translate the patient's ECG waveform into the corresponding symbolic description. Although our own experience with medical doctors—non-specialists—showed that they are quite capable of such a translation, the feeling was that this puts the user into an unusual or unnatural situation. In some practical situations, such manual translation is indeed unfeasible and it has to be mechanized. Available ECG analysis machines could be used to automate this translation step. Most obviously, KARDIO would then be added as a diagnostic expert system to such a machine. Some cardiologists expressed some hesitation regarding this architecture because KARDIO seemed in a way too powerful for such a combination in the view of difficulties in extracting qualitative description features from ECG waveforms. In presently available ECG analysers, these difficulties lead to unreliable recognition of some of the ECG features. However, the integration of a model of KARDIO type into the low-level recognition process would be beneficial also at the low end: it should help to eliminate those low-level interpretations which are impossible with respect to the model. In such a system, KARDIO would then not only serve as a diagnostic expert system, but would also facilitate model-based low-level processing of the ECG signal. This idea has not been developed.

LESSONS LEARNT

There are two main lessons we learned from the KARDIO project, one positive and one negative. On the positive side, we found the approach to knowledge acquisition in KARDIO practical and effective to an extent that in fact surprised even ourselves. The idea of using a logic-based language for qualitative modelling worked very well, and the required specialized reasoning that had to be implemented specifically for the KARDIO model was not much more than an exercise in Prolog programming. This is clearly due to the power of Prolog as an implementation language for other languages and specialized reasoning schemes. The programming itself was never on the critical path in the project.

The strength of the KARDIO approach to qualitative modelling, compared to other approaches, probably lies in the flexibility of the model description language. This language is only restricted to a logic formalism, and does not assume any stronger underlying theory of basic laws or types of constraints for defining the system's dynamics and pattern of behaviour. An essential piece of technology for knowledge acquisition and refinement in KARDIO was also machine learning which we found effective and practical.

On the negative side, the lesson learned was how difficult it is to actually introduce a medical expert system into routine clinical use. There are two main difficulties. One, already mentioned, is mainly concerned with the user interface. That would require direct connection of KARDIO to an ECG electronic instrument which would not require any user intervention. Although we found that potential users, such as general practitioners, were in most cases able to convert the patient's ECG into the symbolic description required by KARDIO, this involvement of a human was considered unsatisfactory by specialist cardiologists and manufacturers of medical instrumentation.

This view appears controversial in the light of the fact, that physicians, non-cardiologists at present have to resort to a superficial guide to 'instant ECG diagnosis'. Such a guide in book form is inferior to KARDIO both with respect to the level of knowledge, and also the flexibility of the use of knowledge. Under these circumstances, KARDIO should be useful even in its present form, without an interface to an ECG device.

However, the lesson learned from the attempts to commercialize KARDIO, is that in addition to the technical merit, the psychological factor is decisive for accepting such a medical expert system into routine practice. The potential manufacturer, also worried about the legal liability, normally consults domain specialists, cardiologists in our case, for opinion. The opinion of the specialists is typically reserved. The reasons for their reservation are in our experience largely irrational and stem from viewing an expert system as a competitor rather than another, in this case 'intelligent', book or manual among many other books that a physician is encouraged to consult to perform the diagnostic task better. Specialists are essentially uninterested in an expert system that can at its best perform like the specialists themselves. They consider an expert system to be a competitor in the task of diagnosis which is by medical specialists believed to be really their exclusive domain. The task of diagnosis is perceived as one requiring highest intellectual skill, experience and intuition, and is impossible to explain and therefore impossible to mechanize. Objective, measurable technical criteria, such as diagnostic accuracy, are of minor importance in this argument. This has been confirmed by a number of other medical diagnostic applications (e.g. Cestnik *et al* 1987). The psychological problem of acceptance was specifically analysed in collaboration with a medical specialist in Zwitter *et al* (1983).

CONCLUSIONS

At the present stage KARDIO consists of several subsystems that support computer diagnosis and prognosis of cardiac arrhythmias. The system could be used as a diagnostic tool in the routine assessment of ECG recordings in preventive or systematic examinations as, by cardiologists' estimation, its performance is equivalent to that of a specialist of internal medicine (non-cardiologist) highly skilled in the reading of ECG recordings. The system could also be used for teaching about electrocardiography in education of all medical profiles. For attaining its practical application the level of detail of the heart model should be more suitably balanced and some changes in the ECG description language would have to be introduced. These changes could be easily introduced within the present framework.

Further work can be directed along various lines including: integration of KARDIO with an ECG analysis machine; extending the model of the heart with treatment of mechanical failures; elaboration of explanation capabilities based on qualitative simulation.

The approach to knowledge acquisition used in the KARDIO project demonstrates that large-scale automatic synthesis of new human-type knowledge is technically feasible. Part of existing cardiological knowledge which is explicitly represented in KARDIO cannot be found in medical literature. The role of the consultant cardiologists who collaborated in the project was not to act as the source of ECG interpretation knowledge to be extracted and incorporated into the ECG diagnostic system, but to help in the design of the logical model of the heart which was then used as a generator of diagnostic rules. The required ECG interpretation knowledge was thus constructed by machine derivation from the compact logical specification.

We expect the KARDIO knowledge acquisition cycle to become a standard technique in the development of practical expert systems. It has already been used in the development of other expert systems, for example at the Turing Institute by Pearce (1988) in a satellite power supply diagnostic system.

REFERENCES

Arity (1986). *The Arity/Prolog Programming Language*. Arity Corporation, Concord, MA.

Bratko, I., Lavrač, N., Mozetič, I., Zrimec, T., Horvat, M. and Rode, P. (1982). *The Development of an Expert System for Intensive Medical Treatment*. Proceedings of the

Technical Conference – Theory and Practice of Knowledge-Based Systems, pp. 5. Brunel University, London.

Bratko, I., Mozetič, I. and Lavrač, N. (1988). Automatic synthesis and compression of cardiological knowledge. In J. Hayes, D. Michie and J. Richards (eds), *Machine Intelligence* 11, Oxford University Press, pp.435–454. Also in Michie, D. and Bratko, I. (eds), *Expert Systems – Automating Knowledge Acquisition. AI Masters Series, Handbook and Video*, Addison Wesley. Reading, MA. pp. 45–61.

Bratko, I., Mozetič, I. and Lavrač, N. (1989). *KARDIO: A Study in Deep and Qualitative Knowledge for Expert Systems*. The MIT Press, Boston, MA.

Cestnik, B., Kononenko, I. and Bratko, I. (1987). Assistant 86: A knowledge-elicitation tool for sophisticated users. In I. Bratko and N. Lavrač (eds), *Progress in Machine Learning*, Sigma Press, Wilmslow.

De Kleer, J. and Brown, J.S. (1983). *The Origin, Form and Logic of Qualitative Physics Laws*. Proceedings of the Eighth International Joint Conference on Artificial Intelligence, Karlsruhe, West Germany. Morgan Kaufmann.

De Kleer, J. and Brown, J.S. (1984). A qualitative physics based on confluences. *Artificial Intelligence*, 24, (1–3), pp.7–83.

Forbus, K.D. (1984). Qualitative process theory. *Artificial Intelligence*, 24, (1–3), pp.85–168.

Goldman, M.J. (1976). *Principles of Clinical Electrocardiography*, Lange Medical Publications, Los Altos.

Grad, A. and Čerček, B. (1984). *Evaluation of the Applicability of the KARDIO-E Expert System*. ISSEK Workshop '84, Bled, Yugoslavia.

Klemenc, M., Mozetič, I. and Ribarič, S. (1984). *An Expert Consultation System for the Use of Antiarrhythmics*. Proceedings of the 8th Bosnian Symposium in Informatics. Jahorina (in Slovene).

Kuipers, B. (1986). Qualitative simulation. *Artificial Intelligence*, 29, pp.289–338.

Lavrač, N. (1984). *KARDIO-E: An Expert System for ECG Diagnosis of Cardiac Arrhythmias*. MSc Thesis, E. Kardelj University, Faculty of Electrical Engineering, Ljubljana, Yugoslavia (in Slovene).

Lavrač, N., Bratko, I., Mozetič, I., Čerček, B., Grad, A. and Horvat, M. (1985). KARDIO-E – An expert system for electrocardiographic diagnosis of cardiac arrhythmias. *Expert Systems: The International Journal of Knowledge Engineering*, 2, pp.46–50.

Michalski, R.S. (1969). *On the Quasi-minimal Solution of the General Covering Problem*. Proceedings of the Fifth International Symposium on Information Processing (FCIP 69), A3 (Switching Circuits), Bled, Yugoslavia, pp.125–128.

Michalski, R.S. and Larson, J. (1975). AQVAL/1 (AQ7) *User's Guide and Program Description*. Report No. 731, University of Illinois at Urbana-Champaign, Department of Computer Science.

Michalski, R.S., Mozetič, I., Hong, J. and Lavrač, N. (1986). *The Multi-purpose*

Incremental Learning System AQ15 and its Testing Application to Three Medical Domains. Proceedings of the AAAI Conference 86, Philadelphia, PA, August 1986. Morgan Kaufmann, St Paul, MA.

Mozetič, I. (1984). *Qualitative Model of the Heart*. Ljubljana: MSc Thesis, E. Kardelj University, Faculty of Electrical Engineering, Ljubljana, Yugoslavia (in Slovene).

Mozetič, I. (1985). NEWGEM: *Program for Learning from Examples – Technical Documentation and User's Guide*. Report, University of Illinois at Urbana-Champaign, Department of Computer Science. Also: Report IJS-DP-4390, Jožef Stefan Institute, Ljubljana.

Mozetič, I. (1986). Knowledge extraction through learning from examples. In T.M. Mitchell, J.G. Carbonell and R.S. Michalski, (eds), *Machine Learning: A Guide to Current Research* Kluwer Academic Publishers, Boston.

Mozetič, I. (1987a). Learning of qualitative models. In I. Bratko and N. Lavrač (eds), *Progress in Machine Learning*. Sigma Press, Wilmslow.

Mozetič, I. (1987b). *The Role of Abstractions in Learning Qualitative Models*. Proceedings of the Fourth International Workshop on Machine Learning, Irvine, CA, June 1987. Morgan Kaufmann, St Paul, MA.

Mozetič, I. (1988). *Learning of Qualitative Models*. PhD Thesis, E. Kardelj University, Faculty of Electrical Engineering, Ljubljana, Yugoslavia (in Slovene).

Mozetič, I., Bratko, I. and Lavrač, N. (1984). *The Derivation of Medical Knowledge from a Qualitative Model of the Heart*. ISSEK Workshop '84, Bled, Yugoslavia.

Pearce, D.A. (1988). The induction of fault diagnosis systems from qualitative models. Proc. National Conference on Artificial Intelligence, AAAI-88, pp. 353–357. Morgan Kaufmann, St Paul, MN.

Pereira, L.M., Pereira, F. and Warren, D.H.D. (1978). *The DEC-system 10 Prolog User's Guide*. University of Edinburgh, Artificial Intelligence Department.

Phibbs, B. (1983). *The Cardiac Arrythmias*. The C.V. Mosby Co., St. Louis.

Zrimec, T., Čerček, B., Rode, P., Lavrač, N., Mozetič, I., Bratko, I., Kononenko, I. and Grad, A. (1983). *An Expert Consultation System for Cardiac Arrhythmias*. Proceedings of the 3rd Mediterranean Conference on Medical and Biological Engineering, Portorož.

Zwitter, M., Bratko, I. and Kononenko, I. (1983). *Rational and Irrational Reservations against the Use of Computer in Medical Diagnosis and Prognosis*. Proceedings of the 3rd Mediterranean Conference on Medical and Biological Engineering, paper 6.4, Portorož.

11

SARTS AutoTest-2

John Ackroff, Pamela Surko,
Gregg Vesonder and Jon Wright

INTRODUCTION

AutoTest-2 (AT-2) was developed at AT & T Bell Laboratories as part of a project to automate the testing and repair of special service circuits. By any operational measure, AT-2 does the job of special services testing successfully on the kind of circuits for which it was designed. It has been well received by the user community, and there are plans to enhance its capabilities in several ways.

Although AT-2 is based on well tested expert system technology (it is written in OPS/83[1] and its principal techniques are forward chaining and match), its most salient feature is that it represents a successful integration of several different programming methodologies. Clearly, expert systems are not the proper solution to all problems. The AT-2 project demonstrates that traditional programming methodologies and expert systems can be successfully integrated in a single application. AT-2 is embedded in a UNIX[2] system based software application called

---

[1] OPS/83 is a trademark of Production System Technologies

[2] UNIX is a registered trademark of AT & T Bell Laboratories

SARTS (Switched Access Remote Test System), which is already widely deployed throughout the United States.

To a large extent, AT-2 is simply another software module running on the SARTS process controller. Much of the challenge of developing AT-2 revolved around fitting AT-2 into the existing SARTS architecture. In particular, an interface between AT-2 and the core SARTS processes was required.

To meet our commitments, we needed an approach that would permit work on the AT-2/SARTS interface and work on the expert system part to proceed in parallel. Our solution was to use prototyping methods to develop the expert system while work on the AT-2/SARTS interface was being completed.

An operational prototype of AT-2 (called PAT-2) was developed which contained the complete expert system engine, but had a non-standard interface to SARTS and a simple user interface. The prototype was surprisingly effective. While it was not a permanent solution, it clearly demonstrated AT-2's potential and gave us an opportunity to receive feedback from users in a realistic setting. Once AT-2's knowledge base was sufficiently complete, it was gracefully embedded into a robust product environment that had been prepared by an independent development effort.

OBJECTIVES

Special services constitute an interesting application domain. There are about 150 different kinds of special services, each with different configurations and different equipment at the ends.

Special services are used, for example, for Automated Teller Machines, host-to-host data communications, and even for some kinds of voice circuits.

Like any telecommunications circuit, special service circuits fail from time to time. When a customer reports trouble with a circuit, human experts test and determine why the circuit is not working. In the Regional Bell Operating Companies (RBOCs), special service testers are supported primarily by SARTS. SARTS provides a database of circuit configurations and other key information, and a human interface for accessing circuits, issuing test commands and receiving measurements. These testers are usually not local to the circuits that are in trouble. It is more economical to have them test from centralized remote locations. Testers located in Dallas, for example, could test circuits in Houston or San Antonio, or could access and test circuits that run between Austin and El Paso.

Circuits may run over a wide geographical area, thus test gear is usually made available at several different places to help a tester localize the trouble. Testing varies in complexity, depending on where and how the test points are wired into the circuit and how the circuit operates.

For example, to decide on a strategy for testing a circuit, it is essential for testers to know how the circuit is configured. In addition, a test measurement that represents trouble on one kind of circuit or configuration may indicate a normal condition on another. Normally, special services testers take six to nine months to complete their training, and much of this time is spent learning about circuit configurations.

AT-2 is intended to test and analyse many of the troubles that testers work on today. When one of these circuits receives a trouble report, a 'test the circuit' command is issued to AT-2. AT-2 executes commands and does analysis in a manner similar to that of expert human testers. The output of AT-2 can easily be read and understood by a human. AT-2 summarizes all actions taken, gives detailed test results, and recommends a disposition for the trouble report (e.g., send out a repair crew, close as 'no trouble found', or send to tester for further analysis).

In operational terms, AT-2 accomplishes two important things. First, testers are saved the manual effort of laboriously collecting all the information they need to understand the troubles on a circuit. Testers rarely need to augment AT-2 output with additional test information. Second, the AT-2 disposition recommendation is often all that is needed to dispatch repair technicians to a trouble site. In these cases, trouble reports are sent immediately out to repair technicians resulting in a high degree of customer responsiveness and increased productivity.

The overall project of which AT-2 is a part is called the *Special Services Automation* project. Special Services Automation speeds the flow of special service trouble reports (and therefore the response to users) by automating trouble report testing, routing, screening, and dispatching. Accurate diagnosis of the troubles on a circuit is essential for effective routing, thus AT-2 is a critical part of the Special Services Automation project.

The most important metrics for AT-2 are tied to the RBOC's repair operations. First, can AT-2 correctly diagnose most troubles (accuracy of diagnosis)? Second, how many trouble reports can AT-2 test during peak periods of operation (busy hour throughput)? Third, how many types of circuits can AT-2 test effectively (coverage)? As we shall see, AT-2 met or exceeded our expectations (and those of the RBOCs) for accuracy, throughput, and coverage.

SYSTEM SPECIFICATION

AT & T Bell Laboratories has a mature development process which includes a careful requirements specification stage. Systems engineering is the discipline which encompasses the art of requirements specification. AT & T has a long history of applying systems engineering to special services operations. Our AT-2 experience suggests that knowledge engineering is a natural extension of traditional systems engineering as it is practised at AT & T Bell Laboratories.

Changes during development

As in most expert systems, the requirements for AT-2 were changed during the system's development. The goal of the prototype was to test both the original specifications and the expert's knowledge in a realistic setting. It also served as an opportunity to demonstrate what could be achieved in the AT-2 product.

In the main, change control was the responsibility of the respective development teams with concurrence of systems engineering. For example, changes that would only affect the rule-based system were approved by systems engineering and the expert systems team. Changes concerning only the AT-2/SARTS interface were reviewed by the SARTS team and systems engineering. Changes that spanned different parts of the system were reviewed by all interested parties before they were installed.

Evaluation criteria

The evaluation criteria were straightforward: the number and kinds of circuits successfully tested, the percentage correctly diagnosed, and the number of test requests processed during the busy hour. The major goal was to correctly diagnose as many problems as possible without human intervention and without major impact on the rest of the SARTS system.

There also were criteria relevant to most large software development projects, e.g. errors per thousand lines of code during unit, integration, system and beta testing. The unit testing was carried out by the developers of a given module using test suites that they personally constructed. Integration testing was a joint effort of the expert system and C development teams. System testing including load testing was done by a separate system testing organization using a carefully constructed battery of tests based on the original system specifications. It was only after AT-2 passed all these tests that it was approved for beta testing at the user's site.

USE OF RESOURCES

An early decision was made to produce both an operational prototype system and a production system. The system would be built by two groups of developers, one group skilled in expert system development and one group skilled in SARTS, UNIX and C development.

The UNIX–C group had many years experience on SARTS development but no experience with expert system development. The responsibility of the C developers was to do all the mainstream code for the product, including user, system and database interfaces. They would not be involved in the construction of the prototype but would concentrate on meeting the downstream goal of producing a product. The developers also understood that during this period they were to acquire skill in building and maintaining expert systems, since they would be responsible for the system's long term maintenance and enhancements.

The expert system developers were veterans who had previously worked on the ACE (Wright *et al* 1988) and OKIES (Gordin *et al* 1988) expert systems. The responsibility of the expert system developers was to do all the rule-based code and the language interface (OPS/83 to C) for the product.

Formal requirements had already been generated for the system by a systems engineer knowledgeable in SARTS and having good relationships with the users and experts in the field. This systems engineer became a key member of the expert system development team. This team was responsible for developing, fielding and supporting both rule-based and conventionally coded parts of the prototype. This was necessary for efficient implementation of refinements along the way. The systems engineer was the first 'expert' to test the system and was the principal intermediary between the experts and the developers.

During the first few months of the project an interface document was produced that specified the nature of the interface between the rule-based and C code to be used in the production system. This specification, periodic meetings and integration 'checkpoints' served as the major mechanisms for keeping the prototype and product groups synchronized.

Even though formal requirements existed, there was a need to test and refine these requirements in the field. It was also important, however, to protect the integrity of the live SARTS system while the prototype was being tested. Therefore the prototype was built on a separate machine and communicated with the SARTS machine (a VAX 11/780) by an asynchronous modem over telephone lines. The hardware chosen was an AT & T 3B2/310 computer. However, the expert system engine would be the same for both the prototype and product architectures.

Prototype software used to simulate the SARTS environment was developed using many of the standard UNIX utilities and a homegrown relational database. The rule-based language was OPS/83, a language well integrated with C, UNIX, and the AT & T 3B2. OPS/83 had been used in a previous expert system (Gordin *et al* 1988) and we had developed several tools including rule-base to database interfaces (Vesonder 1988) that made it easier to develop the system. Thus we had three major reasons for choosing OPS/83: we knew it, we had confidence in it and we had tools that supported it.

INVOLVEMENT OF USERS

One of the unorthodox aspects of this development cycle for us, the developers, was that much of it was done at a user site, i.e. inside a special services centre. The knowledge acquisition stage was, of course, dependent on the collaboration of an expert tester. As soon as we had enough software working to be able to communicate with the automated test gear, we began running tests on some circuits the telephone company has set aside for training new testers. We also began doing a great deal of our programming on site with the expert. The helpfulness of the many experts, coupled with the ease of informal contacts at the coffee pot and over lunch, and 'Hey, Bill?' queries across the lab benches, meant that we were steered away from many mistakes before they happened. When the product was 'ready for testing', it had already seen many hours of use on common circuit configurations.

After several months of testing in an internal special services testing lab, we installed the prototype for a demonstration period in a second Special Services Center. Eventually, the prototype was requested by two other RBOCs and was installed for them as well (making four in all). In exchange for the opportunity to evaluate the product at close hand, the users gave us valuable, detailed feedback on every aspect of the product's operation.

By the time the product version of AT-2 went through its beta test, the prototype had been closely scrutinized and refined by four RBOCs. We were pleased with the results and the reaction of our users in all four RBOCs.

KNOWLEDGE ACQUISITION

Knowledge acquisition for AT-2 consisted of several phases. Our systems engineer had overall responsibility for gathering, distilling, and verifying the knowledge base; the developers used the parts of the knowledge base relevant to their individual parts of the product.

While the systems engineer and the product developers were familiar with special services operations, the expert systems team working on the prototype were not. The first phase of their knowledge acquisition consisted of learning general background information about telephony, special service circuits, the SARTS system, and the operations and work flow in a Special Service Center. This was accomplished by attending training courses intended for new testers and visiting Centers in several of the Regional Bell Operating Companies. The operational information was used to determine where to focus the more intensive knowledge acquisition of the subsequent phases.

Once the prototype development team had acquired some basic knowledge of the domain, the second and most intensive phase of knowledge acquisition began. Several days per week were spent with an expert tester. First, the tester was asked to describe the methods used in special services testing; this included both procedural and decision-making information. This information was used to prepare a document which would serve as the knowledge base. The document was reviewed with the tester and inaccuracies were corrected. Once an initial version of the document was produced, the systems engineer sat with the user during actual testing sessions. Logs and notes from the test sessions were compared to the document, and discrepancies were resolved.

When the document had reached a fairly stable state, it was reviewed with an expert tester from a different RBOC. The systems engineer also spent time with the tester during real test sessions, and they discussed differences between the documented canonical testing procedures and actual practice, just as these differences were discussed with the first expert. Most of the differences between the two experts were in areas that both considered to be 'stylistic'—i.e. they felt that the other's methods were equally valid, but preferred their own methods for idiosyncratic reasons. Only one substantive difference between the experts was found, and this was resolved by consultation with both of them.

At this point, we had a knowledge base that described how expert testers did their jobs. The next, and one of the most crucial phases, was to determine how much of this knowledge could be implemented mechanically, and how well an automated test system would perform. The underlying issue here was that the SARTS system allows testers to listen to troubled circuits while testing and judge the transmission quality by ear. They describe such common problems as cracking, popping, and so on. Much of the trouble identification and isolation is done by listening rather than relying on measurements. Defining an automated test system required the systems engineer and expert tester to rework the knowledge base to describe how a tester who could not monitor the circuit by listening would be able to test effectively. To a certain degree, this was more 'knowledge creation' than knowledge acquisition, since we were describing something that did not exist. Our success here was possible because the earlier knowledge acquisition had tapped the tester's underlying understanding of circuit operation.

The next major phase of knowledge acquisition occurred after the requirements for the product had been written, and constituted yet another verification of the knowledge base. Requirements walk-throughs were held with representatives of several companies, validating our assumptions that the product would be valuable in terms of the amount of the Special Service Center's work that it supported and that the test strategies and analysis procedures were appropriate. Feedback from these reviews was incorporated into the requirements as well.

Feedback from field users of the prototype and early versions of the product provided more input to the knowledge base. Most of this feedback was used to refine the diagnosis part of the product; as users saw the various analysis findings, they were able to suggest ways to combine them to reduce several findings to a single one. This is an important step in realizing the ultimate goal of complete flow-through.

The experts enjoyed participating in the knowledge acquisition process. They appreciated the opportunity to contribute to the design and development of a new feature of the operations system that they use daily in their jobs. They were also surprised to learn that there was so much structure to what they did: they had not previously realized that there was as much rationale to their actions as was uncovered during knowledge acquisition.

REPRESENTATION AND REASONING

The circuit versus the test results

For this task, it might seem obvious that the 'high-level' model one would construct would be that of the circuit. A circuit connects equipment at point A with other equipment at point Z. It consists of a series of legs, attached to each other through connection points. The database entry describing the circuit gives configuration information about what equipment comprises the circuit, and where the available test points are. One could, as one sectionalized the circuit looking for the type and location of the problem, mark each leg with the results of the tests, and whether the tests show the part of the circuit to be within or outside of specifications. As testing progressed, more and more information would become known about the circuit. Eventually, all problem(s) are isolated, or every part of the circuit is shown to be trouble free.

In fact, it seems that this is not the model used by the expert testers. They model their analysis on a (growing) set of consistent or inconsistent test results or measurements. In other words, the key concept underlying the problem space is the tester's notion of what test results are needed to adequately make a judgement about the circuit. These test results are labelled with the testpoint at which they were done, and in what direction the measurements were made (e.g. at test point 1, looking toward the 'A' end of the circuit). Each segment of a circuit has a characteristic test 'signature' or pattern of results. Similarly, faults on that same segment have their own identifiable pattern.

The tester's job is complicated by the fact that the circuit itself may be made up of pieces belonging to different companies, and the tester may not be able to test all the pieces, or even to know what equipment comprises the parts of the circuit not belonging to the tester's company. The set of test results is something the tester has control over and is responsible for. Occasionally, testers may use the test results to 'guess' about what equipment is on the circuit in these situations in order to develop an appropriate strategy.

In order to ease communication with the experts, AT-2 reasons about test results, not about circuits. To a large extent, AT-2 is a sophisticated classifier of test results.

The advantages of focusing on test results are obvious: knowledge acquisition was made easier and more accurate, and the determination of faults or satisfactory performance through signature analysis was direct and natural.

Control

The control strategy employed was mainly simple forward chaining and match. We used two special control conventions. To handle the sequential aspects of the task (get a circuit, retrieve its characteristics from the database, run tests, report tests to the results database) we stepped through stages of a finite state machine by deleting a (single) *stage* working memory element and replacing it with the next one once all work relating to that stage was complete.

The task of testing was described to us by the experts as basically a decision tree, with some shortcuts. We used a subroutine convention to walk this decision tree. Each interior node on the decision tree pushed the 'goals' (actually work stages) necessary to visit its children. It popped its own 'goal' when its work and that of its children were complete. These two control strategies were all that were needed to handle the flow of control for all types of circuits tested.

We attempted to bring all facts and local parameters into the program as table entries, to make the program as customizable as possible. In addition, since we felt that signature analysis would continue to become more sophisticated, the rules activated for a given signature were also governed by entries in a table, even though this table was not accessible to users.

The nature of the domain means that we needed very little sophistication in handling uncertainty. We recognized that it is possible to get inconsistent test results. The users were pleased to have a system that 'knows when it doesn't know', that is, one that points out inconsistencies when they occur, and does not automatically dispatch repair crews in these cases. A human then reviews the results, and bases a decision on information unavailable to the program—usually specialized, local knowledge, perhaps representing temporary conditions and often applicable to only one site.

Size

There were about 650 rules in AT-2 when the first version was complete. As is true of other operational expert systems, this number continuously changes, and more rules are being added as AT-2 is enhanced in both the types of circuits it is able to test and in the sophistication of its testing.

In addition to the rules, there were roughly 400 'facts', or local parameters. Facts were in general very simple pieces of information, and were usually brought in as table entries, so that they could be customized by each special services centre. A fact might be the noise level at which a circuit changes from 'okay' to 'marginally noisy', or the classes of conclusions for which the company would like the results screened by a human before dispatching a work crew.

USER INTERFACE

Interfaces were provided for basic users, advanced users, and administrators. For each class of user, the interface was designed to be consistent with the existing SARTS system as much as possible.

This being the case, most of the interaction with the AT-2 feature is accomplished by filling out 'masks' on block-mode synchronous terminals. Some new masks were created, and some existing masks were changed. For example, new fields were added to a circuit database to support AT-2; the mask used to manage the records in this database was changed to allow users to enter, view, and change the values of these fields.

The 'basic user' interface was designed to allow people with little or no testing knowledge to request circuit tests. The 'advanced user' interface is similar; it allows the user to view the testing strategies 'recommended' by a table managed by the administrator and to override these recommendations if the user believes them to be inappropriate.

Note that in both cases, the interface allows the user to request a test, and to retrieve the results at a later time. AT-2 does not interact with the user while it tests.

The administrative interface provides control over how the feature operates. Administrators can assign default testing strategies based on criteria such as the type of circuit being tested (e.g. data as opposed to voice), whether the circuit has had chronic troubles etc. Administrators can specify the action limits used in interpreting measurements as well as the messages that are used in the test report to describe various findings.

EVALUATION

Based on results from several early trial sites, we feel that we have met or exceeded our objectives. We produced an automated testing system for special service circuits which handles about the same amount of work in the Special Services Center as projected by our early estimates. Throughput is well within acceptable limits, and the findings are accurate enough so that most troubles can be resolved with no further testing. Machine resources have been managed so that, even during the 'busy hour' there are enough resources left to deliver acceptable response time to the human users of the system.

Examination of just a subset of the results from one of the initial trials gives an insight into the true potential of AT-2. In this centre, which is responsible for approximately 35 000 circuits, 46% of the customer-reported troubles are on data circuits. AT-2 is used to test all of these circuits; 80% of the troubles are able to be resolved without any further testing. In some cases, the tester must do more analysis, interpreting AT-2's measurement results with circuit configuration information from an external database; in many cases, the work is forwarded to the appropriate repair crew based solely on the analyses and diagnoses provided by AT-2.

There is a saving not only in the amount of labour needed on the trouble but also in customer response time—the time needed to restore a properly-working circuit to the customer once a trouble report is received. Testers typically spend about half an hour either assembling the information they need to test or doing actual testing; the average test time for AT-2 tested data circuits in the Special Services Center that was evaluated was six minutes—a substantial improvement.

Factoring together AT-2's reliability (in terms of its ability to diagnose correctly many types of circuit failures, as well as to know when a circuit is working correctly) with the time savings available and total number of Special Service circuits, we estimate that AT-2 represents potential annual savings in the tens of millions of dollars range nationwide.

Most of the changes made and planned based on the early field trials have been enhancements in the diagnosis phase of AT-2. We plan to expand the scope of the product by extending coverage to additional types of circuits; we are also investigating changing some of the measurement procedures to provide more valid measurements. In including new test strategies to support additional testing some design changes have been identified; these changes will allow on-going design to proceed more quickly than the old design, but do not require the existing code to be rewritten.

Perhaps the most significant aspect of our AT-2 experience is that we also demonstrated that we could incorporate an expert system into an existing 'conventional-software-based' operations system. We view this as an example of our ability to match technology and applications appropriately, and to use that technology in a way that benefits us and our users.

At the end of 1988, AT-2 was running in five Special Services Centers throughout the United States. Two RBOCs have indicated their intent to deploy the product throughout their companies, and other companies were planning to start trials in 1989.

ORGANIZATIONAL ISSUES

The expert system project started as a response to a competitive need for a timely introduction of a product into the marketplace. Our users were pressing their vendors to develop the software quickly. In response to this need the project managers decided to augment the main development team with additional developers skilled in expert system development.

The need for an early working prototype that could be modified to reflect the expert's wishes resulted in the selection of the expert system approach, even though it was recognized that the system could be developed using mainstream techniques.

This decision was made with some reservations. There was no precedent at AT & T for integrating expert systems within such a large software system and the expert system developers were not originally part of the tightly knit SARTS team. SARTS has been deployed since 1978, with continuing on-going development and enhancements. The system has a well deserved reputation among its users for its stability and high quality. The SARTS developers wanted to use new technology in this system. In response to these concerns, a plan was developed to test the progress of the system at regular intervals. In addition, there were regular meetings with several levels of concerned management to check for any potential pitfalls and solve them as quickly as possible.

During the prototyping stage of the product, the C developers and expert system developers worked relatively independently. The goal of the ES developers was to field the prototype as quickly as possible. The C developers were working on their parts of the system for the product. During the initial stages when the interface specifications were produced the goal was to lift the ES code from the prototype and slip it in the space provided by the C developers. (Surprisingly, by and large, that is what happened!)

After the prototype was fielded, integration with the product began. This time was also used to begin the technology transfer to the SARTS C developers. Courses on OPS/83 and rule-based programming were presented by the expert system developers and, as the developers became more comfortable with the system, the SARTS developers interned with the expert system developers to solve problems that occurred. Within a few months the C developers soloed on rule-based programming and currently are maintaining and enhancing the AT-2 system using rule-based and other technologies.

LESSONS LEARNED

Our AT-2 experience has confirmed our beliefs on three important issues. They are (1) being able to integrate expert systems into existing software applications, (2) the use of prototyping as a software methodology, and (3) the need to plan for migration from prototype to product. Our overall success was achieved only through our realization of these three goals.

Integration with existing systems

AT-2 is closely integrated with SARTS and is part of a family of systems that will automate trouble report processing for special services. We think that the ability to integrate expert systems with conventional software applications will become increasingly important.

Many computer systems developed in the recent past attacked problems that were highly complex and multi-faceted. Completely automated solutions were not, in general, possible. Successful systems addressed those parts of a problem that could be automated economically, but left the difficult and intractable parts to people. Doing the complete job was really the result of a partnership between machines and people. Many systems provided computerized reports or displays that made the jobs of their human partners easier.

SARTS is a good example of this kind of system. Some parts of the special services testing job have been automated, but others are assigned to people. Doing the total job requires that both people and machines do their parts correctly. To help people do their part, SARTS has a sophisticated user interface that graphically depicts the state of circuit while it is being tested. Testers enter commands and see their effects directly in front of them.

Expert systems, however, are bringing a wider range of problems into the domain of automation. Consequently, it is becoming possible to automate some pieces of these complex software applications that previously did not have economically feasible solutions. In some sense, the existing computer systems (like SARTS) form a base on which these new applications can be developed.

AT-2 gives us a good example. AT-2 would not have been possible without a complex base of application software in SARTS that managed access and operation of the installed test equipment. By the same token, AT-2 extends SARTS beyond its original capabilities.

The importance of prototyping

Prototyping has a role to play in many kinds of software development, not just expert systems. In our case, the principal advantage of prototyping was that both developers and system engineers became closely involved with the application and consequently were able to make good decisions regarding AT-2's functionality.

PAT-2—the prototype version of AT-2—had other important effects. It not only enhanced our understanding of special services testing, but it convinced our users, our management, and, to some extent, ourselves, that an expert system for special services testing could be successful. The existence of PAT-2 gave us confidence that we were moving in the right direction. PAT-2 had a very significant and positive effect on the project.

As a result of this experience, we have come to believe that the techniques and methodology developed by the artificial intelligence community have potential as general prototyping techniques. AI methods seldom require the developer to have a complete understanding of an application before beginning development. In fact, program development itself is sometimes used as an exercise that enhances the developer's understanding of the key issues. This is an important advantage, because rarely is an application adequately understood in the early stages of a prototype.

In addition, AI methods encourage the developer to focus on getting the functionality right rather than on specific implementation issues. The formalization of program organization as search through a problem space, or as knowledge that must be represented in data structures and properly organized, has the effect of bringing home the importance of the application. We believe that this emphasis gives the developer a better chance of arriving at the right functionality for a new system.

Having viable paths from prototype to product

In our view, expert system projects fail too frequently because they cannot escape the prototype stage. The most frequent reason is a failure on the part of the developers to provide a viable migration path to product. The time between the completion of the prototype and the availability of the product version is the key variable.

This is partly a function of the programming environments and software tools selected for the prototype effort. We strongly favour UNIX-based tools because UNIX provides a base of conventional software tools that can be used in a prototype and yet can be converted easily into a production environment. Conversion of prototypes developed in LISP machine environments is just too great an obstacle to overcome, no matter how useful or valuable the prototype. The conversion effort can sometimes exceed the effort needed to develop the prototype.

Other elements are equally important. For example, failure to plan early for transfer of technology can be devastating for an expert systems project. In addition, system administration, training, documentation, and tools for system test must be provided, just as in any software development project. Our own experience tells us that much of the work needed to develop an expert system is highly conventional in nature—perhaps as much as 70% of a successful expert systems application uses conventional techniques.

The delay between the completion of a prototype system and the availability of a product version is critical to success for several reasons. Having seen a working prototype, users are usually ill-prepared to understand the reasons for a lengthy conversion process. In addition, competitors may be waiting to capitalize on product delays. As a prototype, by its nature, is more or less public, it is an excellent source of ideas that can be easily exploited.

AT-2 was successful partly because the delay between prototype and product versions was relatively short. In fact, the period between the completion of the prototype and the start of beta test for the product was a few months. The product version of AT-2 was available about nine months after the prototype was completed.

CONCLUSIONS

AT-2 uses well established expert system techniques, but still accomplishes some interesting things. By any operational measure, AT-2 does the job of special services testing successfully. To say that it has been well received by the user community may understate the case. There are plans to enhance its capabilities in many different ways. These plans suggest that AT-2 will be a viable product for years to come.

AT-2 was a key piece in a large family of systems making up the *Special Services Automation* strategy. Expert systems technology, therefore, was entrusted with an important role in a much larger project, and came through.

The transfer of technology to new developers, initially unfamiliar with expert systems, was successful. All new development, enhancements, and maintenance is now their responsibility.

Finally, we believe that AT-2 represents a successful integration of several different programming methodologies. It is not our view that expert systems are the solution to all problems. Most real-world complex applications require the successful fitting together of technologies that suit different aspects of an application. Expert systems, applied to the right problems, can be used profitably in many traditional software applications.

REFERENCES

Gordin, D., Foxvog, D., Rowland, J., Surko, P. and Vesonder, G. (1988). *OKIES: A Troubleshooter in the Factory*. The First International Conference on Industrial and Engineering Applications of Artificial Intelligence and Expert Systems, 1988, Tullahoma, TN.

Vesonder, G. (1988). Rule-based programming in the UNIX system. *AT & T Technical J.*, 1988, pp.69–80.

Wright, J. R., Zielinski, J. E. and Horton, E. M. (1988). Expert Systems development: the ACE system. In J. Liebowitz (ed.), *Expert System Applications to Telecommunications*, Wiley, New York.

REFERENCES

Dowling, D., Looyog, D., Rowland, L., Surko, R. and Vaughan, C. (1986) OKES: A Rule-based Tool for ... in The First International Conference on Industrial and Engineering Applications of Artificial Intelligence and Expert Systems, 1988, Tullahoma, TN.

Wandke, C. (1988) Rule-based programming in the UNIX system. AI @ T Technical J., 1988, pp.69-80.

Wright, J. R., Zielinski, T. E. and Horton, E. M. (1988) Expert Systems development: the ACE system. In J. Liebowitz (ed.), Expert System Applications to Telecommunications, Wiley, New York.

Index

Index compiled by Dawn Bramer